Society
Schools
and
Learning

Society
Schools
and
Learning

WILBUR B. BROOKOVER

Professor of Education and Sociology
Michigan State University

EDSEL L. ERICKSON

Associate Professor of Sociology and Education
Western Michigan University

Allyn and Bacon, Inc.   Boston

Library of Congress Catalog Card Number: 71-77899.
Printed in the United States of America.

Preface

UNTIL QUITE RECENTLY scientists and educators have tended to ignore the contributions that social forces make to a person's ability to learn. This book is an effort to encourage an awareness and concern for how a student's ability to learn, as well as what he learns, is shaped by the social context within which he functions. This book is also designed to acquaint the reader with historical and contemporary perspectives of learning and how certain of these perspectives have helped to maintain dysfunctional aspects of our educational system.

As a college text, this book is appropriate for students in social foundations of education, sociology of education, and social-psychology of education courses. It may also supplement curriculum and educational psychology courses where attention is given to the social context of learning.

Our thanks must go to many persons for making this book possible. We are indebted to our research colleagues and friends whose ideas permeate our work: Jean LePere, Don Hamachek, and Keith Anderson, Michigan State University; Shailer Thomas, The Ohio State University; Lee Joiner, Southern Illinois University; Ann Paterson, University of West Virginia; Richard Towne, The State University of New York, Buffalo; Richard Morse, Stillman College, and Terry Schurr, Ball State University.

We are also appreciative of the valued editorial assistance received from Jack Peters and Beverly Malatesta of Allyn and Bacon, Inc. and Josephine Wharton and Ruth Jennings, our secretaries.

Finally, we are grateful to our wives Edna Brookover and Ruth Erickson for their intelligent assistance.

WBB
ELE

Contents

1. THE SOCIAL CONTEXT OF LEARNING   1

     INTELLIGENCE AND ITS MEASUREMENT   3

     ALTERNATE THEORIES OF INTELLIGENCE   13

     SUGGESTED READINGS   17

2. SOCIETY, CULTURE, AND EDUCATION   19

     SOCIETY AND CULTURE   20

     THE TRANSMISSION OF CULTURE   26

     SUGGESTED READINGS   39

3. SUB-CULTURAL VARIATION AND EDUCATION   40

     SUB-CULTURAL GOALS OF EDUCATION   41

     EDUCATIONAL POLICY AND CULTURAL DIVERSITY   44

     SUB-CULTURAL VARIATIONS IN THE UNITED STATES   46

     SUB-CULTURAL DIVERSITY AND SCHOOL LEARNING   56

     SUGGESTED READINGS   62

4. GROUP NORMS AND EXPECTATIONS   64

     TYPES OF GROUPS   64

     THE IDENTIFICATION OF
     STUDENTS' SIGNIFICANT OTHERS   68

THE SCHOOL SOCIAL SYSTEM   80

IMPLICATIONS FOR EDUCATION   93

SUGGESTED READINGS   97

5. THE SELF IN RELATION TO OTHERS   99

SELF-CONCEPTS IN RELATION TO ROLE   101

THE IMPACT OF PARENTS
AND TEACHERS ON SELF-CONCEPT   107

SUGGESTED READINGS   113

6. RACE, CLASS, AND EDUCATION   115

SEGREGATION VS. EQUALITY OF
OPPORTUNITY IN AMERICAN EDUCATION   116

TYPES OF SCHOOL SEGREGATION   119

RECENT CHANGES IN SEGREGATION POLICY   121

THE EFFECTS OF SEGREGATION   127

EDUCATION OF STUDENTS
DISADVANTAGED BY RACE AND CLASS   134

SUGGESTED READINGS   137

7. EDUCABILITY AND THE FUTURE SOCIETY   138

INDEX   143

The
Social
Context
of
Learning

IN ORDER TO UNDERSTAND the educational process in any society, we must first understand the social environment within which learning occurs. Many teachers are aware that the social environment of any student somehow influences the knowledge, values, and behavior which he learns in or out of school. Unfortunately, however, other beliefs often obscure the importance of the social context for learning. There are few teaching theories in vogue which take into account a sophisticated understanding of how the social environment influences what and how much is learned by students. The purpose of this book is to present a series of ideas about how social forces may influence student behavior—particularly academic behavior.

Nearly all human behavior is learned or acquired in association with other human beings. In this sense, the entire educational process involves the interaction of the individual with other persons, groups, and complex social organizations in his social environment. In the following chapters, we shall

1

examine how several aspects of the social environment affect the learning of human behavior with particular emphasis on learning in school.

In Chapter 2, we shall examine how the broad general categories which we commonly term "society" and "culture" are related to the similarities and differences in behavior acquired by the members of each society. In Chapter 3, we shall turn to the effect of different segments or divisions of the total society on the process of learning and the kinds of behavior acquired. These segments are commonly identified as *sub-societies* or *sub-cultures*. In this section we shall discuss regional, rural-urban, ethnic, racial, and social class differences in American society and their relation to the educational process. Because of the current concern we shall pay particular attention to the lower-class sub-society or- sub-culture commonly identified as *the disadvantaged*. In Chapter 6, we shall further analyze the educational policy and practice which is relevant to the equality of educational opportunity for the disadvantaged.

The third general category of social phenomena with which we shall be concerned may be identified as *social organizations* or groups of various sizes. These are generally smaller in size than sub-cultural categories and may cut across various such categories. At the smaller group level, we shall identify the patterns of interaction and impact of particular individuals which have major importance for the student. We identify these as *significant others*.

The fourth aspect of our analysis focuses on the individual and his perception of how he should and can behave in a particular arena of behavior. The individual's behavior is structured by his interaction with others in the social environment. We shall, however, go somewhat beyond this formulation and examine the process by which the individual develops perceptions of himself and recognizes what is appropriate and proper for him in his society. We shall explore the significance of this with particular reference to the processes of learning in the school situation.

Many of the ideas discussed are well known to educators and behavioral scientists, but they have generally not been applied to the operation of the educational system. The primary emphasis in the schools has been on individual learning ability and the processes by which the individual learns. Perhaps this results from the fact that our beliefs about learning ability and the processes of education developed during a period in which human behavior was largely explained in organic terms. The belief that differences in academic achievement are best explained by differences in capacity to learn, which are relatively fixed, is still carefully nurtured in many schools and universities. Before we undertake an analysis of other social forces which influence academic performance, we shall examine contemporary beliefs about learning ability and why these beliefs have persisted in Western education.

INTELLIGENCE AND ITS MEASUREMENT

Perhaps the most important among the many social forces affecting learning are the beliefs about the nature of learning ability which prevail in a society, i.e. how people define intelligence. The prevailing conceptions of intelligence in our society are (1) that ability to learn is relatively fixed or unchangeable, and (2) that it is predetermined by heredity. These beliefs assume that each individual has a limited ability to learn and that this ability is unaffected by external social forces. Another common assumption is that the fixed ability of individuals can be measured with reasonable accuracy by intelligence tests. We shall examine the inadequacy of these beliefs about ability and the reasons for their persistence in spite of evidence which has not supported them.

Over the past several decades much research has sought to determine the stability of intelligence and the relative impact of inheritance and environment on intelligence. After a careful review and reinterpretation of the research relevant to fixed intelligence and its predetermined development, J.

McV. Hunt, in *Intelligence and Experience*, summarizes his findings and interpretations:

Intelligence has been a topic of central concern for those seeking to understand human nature. Even though tests of intelligence and of the aptitudes derived therefrom have been of more practical help than tests of any kind in selecting people for quality performance in various situations, discussions of intelligence have typically been marked by polemics. These polemics have usually concerned two of the beliefs or assumptions about intelligence that have dominated thought on the topic from the turn of the twentieth century through World War II. According to these two dominant assumptions, intelligence is fixed and immutable, and the development of the individual's basic repertoire of responses and capacities is predetermined by his heredity.

The implications of these two assumptions spilled over in various directions. Intelligence came to be defined as "inherited capacity," and it was looked upon as a basic dimension of an individual person. The hope of improving a man's lot was shifted from the euthenic strategy of improving his upbringing and education to the eugenic strategy of finding some way to select only the more intelligent for the propagation of the race. Differential fertility came to be viewed with alarm. Investigative effort concerning child nature and child development was directed toward the normative mode of measuring the individual characteristics and relating the measures of age. Individual characteristics were quantified and discussed in the language of *dimensions* and *scales* without ascertaining their development and neuropsychological characteristics. Investigations of the effects of various kinds of experience at various ages on the development of intellectual capacity were discouraged. Practical educational efforts to cultivate intellectual capacity, particularly in the very young, were discouraged. With behavioral development conceived to be a process in which anatomic maturation automatically brought with it the response repertoire, experts warned parents not to overstimulate their infants but rather to leave them alone to grow. Finally the assumptions of fixed intelligence and predetermined development may well have had something to do with what has probably been an over-emphasis upon personal selection and an underemphasis upon problems of both training and arranging the social climate of institutions to foster personal interest and growth.[1]

In spite of this scientifically based knowledge demonstrating that intelligence test scores vary with experiences and change under certain circumstances, many persons have continued to believe that intelligence is a constant and fixed quantity largely predetermined in the organism. Over the years, evidence contrary to a belief in fixed learning ability has been ignored or discounted by the great body of educational theorists and by most practitioners in American schools. Measurement and testing specialists in American universities and in the school systems generally are fully aware of the evidence and have generally emphasized that intelligence and other related aptitude measures are sample measures of what the individual has learned and do not measure directly any fixed or inherited capacity or ability. However, the assumption of fixed ability continues to dominate the practice and organization of American education. The emphasis on the identification of people with various learning "abilities" or "talents," and through this the selection of people for various types of education and training, have overshadowed any efforts in American schools to cultivate the appropriate social climates or environments which would develop the academic abilities of children in appropriate fields. The emphasis is, therefore, on identifying and selecting, so that the round pegs are appropriately placed in the round holes, rather than on creating the appropriate environment and providing the experience that would produce the kind of citizens needed in a highly technical and literate society. We must investigate the reasons for this continued assumption of fixed ability in order to understand and improve our educational system.

[1] Reprinted from J. McVicker Hunt, *Intelligence and Experience*, pp. 347-348, by permission of the publishers (copyright © 1961, The Ronald Press Company).

Historical Development of Fixed
Intelligence Concept

The concept of intelligence or mental traits had its origin in the latter half of the nineteenth century when the science of genetics was emphasizing biological processes and developing the determination of characteristics through the genes. Francis Galton's early work entitled *Hereditary Genius*[2] and his later work in 1883 on the inquiries into human faculty[3] were among the foundation treatises in the development of the notion of heredity and fixed intelligence. Alfred Binet, to whom we have turned for outstanding contributions in the development of intelligence tests, did not contend that intelligence was fixed.

In response to those who maintained that the intelligence of an individual was constant, Binet indicated "a child's mind is like a field for which an expert farmer has advised a change in the method of cultivating, with the result that in place of desert land, we now have a harvest. It is in this particular sense, the one which is significant, that we say that the intelligence of children may be increased."[4]

Hunt maintains that one of the reasons for our acceptance of the Galton biological theories of intelligence instead of the postulates of Binet is that the idea of using tests particularly in the schools was brought to America by Cattell who had been a student of Galton rather than a student of Binet.[5]

However, we must also recognize that the development of intelligence-testing and the complex of beliefs about intelligence had its origin and early development in a period when human behavior generally was being explained in terms of relatively fixed inherited characteristics. Throughout the nine-

[2] Francis Galton, *Hereditary Genius, An Inquiry into its Laws and Consequences* (London: Macmillan, 1869).

[3] Francis Galton, *Inquiries into Human Faculty and its Development* (London: Macmillan, 1883).

[4] Alfred Binet, *Les Idées Modernes sur les enfants.* (Paris: Ernest Flarnarion, 1909). Cited in G. D. Stoddard, "The IQ: Its Ups and Downs." *Educational Research*, 1939, 20:44-57.

[5] Hunt, *op. cit.*, pp. 13-14. The discussion of reasons for persistence of the belief in fixed intelligence draws heavily on Hunt.

teenth century and the early decades of the twentieth century, instincts were the predominant explanation of differences in human behavior. These were essentially fixed behavioral patterns determined by hereditary processes. It is not surprising, therefore, that mental processes were conceived as an inherited phenomenon like color of eyes or color of skin. Binet's belief about the improvability of intelligence and his protest against "this brutal pessimism" was not likely to be widely accepted when the predominant mode of thinking and explanation of human characteristics and behavior was based on heredity with statically fixed dimensions.

Intelligence as a Concept with Dimensions of Quantity

The concept of a fixed or constant hereditary intelligence is closely associated with the concept of quantity. With the development of attempts to measure or determine the extent of intelligence, the measuring devices or *scales* had to be applied to something. As Hunt indicates, "The application of such terms as dimension or scale may at once tend to carry their meaning in the physical world over to . . . behavior and to imply that the concept of constancy of dimensions is being generalized from static objects to non-static persons and their behavior."[6] It is not easy and perhaps did not seem logical to try to measure a concept that was changing and in the process of developing. It seemed relatively meaningless to measure something that at another time was going to be different. Since the early efforts of Galton and others to measure intelligence were associated with the retarded or the "feebleminded," investigators were concerned with identifying those people with limited or inadequate amounts of whatever was being measured. Thus, the whole semantics and logic associated with intelligence were concerned with dimensions of amount or quantity of the subject being tested or measured. Our vocabulary dealing with intelligence has consequently come to presuppose some fixed amount to which a scale might be applied.

[6] *Ibid.*, p. 309.

Metaphorically, we have identified this fixed conception of learning ability as the "bucket" theory of intelligence. The metaphor makes it possible to perceive of individuals as having varying capacities, potentials, or quantities which might be measured in terms of some scale. Associated with quantity and dimension is the conception of limits: the individual who has a small quantity or small dimension for learning cannot expand the size of his bucket. In most discussions of the goals of education, educational leaders tend to emphasize the importance of educating the individual to the *limits* of *his capacity*.

College and university administrators talk about educating anyone who has the potential or who can profit by such experience. Such discussion reflects the notion of dimension or quantity. Although we know that the contemporary intelligence and aptitude tests do not measure such dimensions, our vocabulary is associated with the concept of a fixed and measurable dimension or quantity. Furthermore, intelligence tests are generally used by educators to estimate how much potential—how large a bucket—a particular student has. However, we have no vocabulary which posits the concept of change or expansion or development of intelligence through the creation of appropriate environmental experiences. The concept of a varying and pliable learning ability is therefore very difficult to introduce, and it is not easy for us to comprehend such an idea without a vocabulary with which to discuss it.

Convenience for Measurement

The notion of fixed intelligence, in fact, the entire history and theory of intelligence, has been associated with the process of measuring intelligence as an entity within the individual. Hunt suggests that psychologists and others who deal with measurement in the schools are more likely to maintain that intelligence is a fixed and constant factor than those psychologists who are concerned with learning, personality, or social behavior. Hunt is here suggesting that the perpetuation of the theory of fixed intelligence is in part a function of the faith which many measurement psychologists in private and public practice wish to perpetuate. The convenience for them in assuming a static quantity or dimension was such that so long as the psychologist was professionally identified with the testing function "it was highly comforting to believe that the characteristics tested were fixed in individuals. Evidence hinting that the characteristics might not be fixed produced intense dissonance, for it threatened both his belief in fixity and the adequacy of his professional function as well. Such a factor may help to explain the sometimes excessive violence of the polemics concerning the constancy of the IQ and the effects of early training that were common in the years just previous to World War II."[7] The threat of the conception of variable learning abilities depending on environment and experience was therefore unconsciously affecting the acceptance or rejection of data provided by the measurement specialists' own research.

Explanation for School Failure

As the emphasis on common education increased in American society, both parents and teachers became more concerned about the effectiveness of the teaching and the success of the student in acquiring prescribed knowledge. Prior to the advent of the concept of intelligence, the responsibility for failure to learn in school was ascribed to either the child's willful abstinence or the teacher's incompetence. The concept of fixed and limited intelligence excused both from any responsibility. The teacher could without any guilt whatsoever explain that a given child did not have the necessary intelligence to acquire a particular body of knowledge or to learn a particular type of behavior. The child was likewise absolved of any responsibility. In fact, the associated belief was developed that it was dangerous for the teacher to impose knowledge or skills on a child who did not have the necessary capacity or intelligence. The parents might be somewhat disturbed at first, but they also were absolved of responsibility because they did not know of the limited capacity which their inheritance would produce.

[7] *Ibid.*, pp. 14-15.

Contemporary Need for Education

The concept of fixed and *limited* ability also fitted the needs of American society during the early decades of the twentieth century. Only a small proportion of the society needed to have high levels of education. When the program of universal education was established in the country, it provided the minimal necessary education for all children. The task of the schools was then to select a limited proportion of students for high-school education and then select some of these for further education in medicine, law, ministries, engineering, and later, teaching. The great majority of the youth was expected to be and in fact was absorbed in agricultural occupations and the limited range of business activities which were necessary in the rural society. As industrialization occured, the vast majority of the workers in industry needed only limited skill and required relatively limited educational prerequisites.

During that period, educators were concerned about educating too many youth to such high levels that many could not find positions commensurate with their education. The justification therefore for limiting the level of education of the great majority may have been appropriate in the period of rural and early industrial development. At any rate, the assumption of fixed and limited capacities was an effective device (if not valid) for justifying the selection of a limited number of persons for advanced education.

A combination of the pressure for more education in the 1920's and 1930's and the concern about the employment of children in industry resulted in the rapid expansion of high-school educational opportunities. Since it was assumed that only a limited number of children had the fixed abilities for the traditional or pre-professional high-school education, the educational programs were adapted to meet the needs of these particular students and to train needed personnel for the society. Vocational education in agriculture, home economics, commercial and industrial skills, as well as an industrial arts program, were developed to educate the boys and girls who were needed in these vocational areas as well as to justify their remaining in school when they were "unable to learn the academic subjects."

During the third and fourth decades of the twentieth century, the selection of students for post high-school education became a primary function of the secondary school program. Although we now justify the selection process as a means of predicting the child's success in a particular curriculum or an advanced educational program, the process developed in a period when there was little concern with prediction; rather the selection process was based on the assumption that one needed to identify the extent and type of capacities possessed by each individual. The use of intelligence and related tests had their great growth during this period.

The Testing Technology

The needs of the society and the assumptions of fixed intelligence converged to promote the use of a vast complex of tests and related devices for the identification of people with varying abilities and the prediction of success in various types of educational programs. The entire complex of aptitude, intelligence, and interest-testing programs was designed to fit the round pegs into the round holes and the square pegs into the square holes. The technology, of course, has been expanded beyond the educational system into the whole process of personnel selection in business, industry, and government. Although tests have not been able to account for more than 25 or 30 per cent of the variance in performance in later levels of education and even less in various types of jobs, the technology has persisted and expanded. A whole new profession of measurement specialists in the schools and universities and a vastly profitable industry developed to standardize and service the testing complex in American education. Although sophisticated testing specialists have long recognized that their devices do not measure any innate intelligence or capacities, many test users continue to assume a relatively fixed or static quantity. As we noted earlier, Hunt[8] and other measurement

[8] *Ibid.*

people found it difficult to rationalize their professional activities without tacitly assuming a constant dimension for intelligence or other traits which they were measuring.

Many users of intelligence and other aptitude-measurement devices are less sophisticated in what the devices measure and have generally continued to use tests as if they were measuring some fixed capacity or dimension.

The Norms of the Education-Social System

Research tends to support the thesis that even the intelligence which we measure varies with the social and other environmental factors over a period of time. A recent longitudinal study of secondary school students reveals that the measured intelligence of this age group changes greatly from one period to another. The California Test of Mental Maturity scores of approximately 70 per cent of this population changed significantly from the ninth grade to the eleventh grade.[9] In spite of the evidence on variation and change in measured intelligence, the beliefs have persisted.

Although we cannot go into the literature on social change at this point, it is well established that social norms and values tend to persist even though they may become dysfunctional to their social systems. In the case of the educational system and its beliefs concerning fixed intelligence, we have a highly integrated system which functioned extremely well in the American society for several decades. Our belief in fixed intelligence may persist because it makes many of us feel better about what we are doing in the schools. The placement of children in special classes, and schools for the trainable or educable mentally retarded, and the assignment of presumably normal-range children in slow groups or curricula has the effect in many cases of limiting or denying the educational opportunities of these children. The belief that they have fixed

---

[9] W. B. Brookover *et. al., Self-Concept of Ability and School Achievement III* (Educational Publication Services, College of Education, East Lansing: Michigan State University, 1967).

and limited capacities to learn and therefore cannot benefit from other educational programs may make some feel better about the practice.

Perhaps the polemics which characterize discussions about fixed intelligence are a reflection, for some, of an emotional attachment for a set of beliefs. This analysis of the reasons for the persistence of our belief system is not intended to cast any criticism on any particular group of educators or specialists in our educational-social system. On the contrary, it should emphasize the integration of a social system which served the needs of American society extremely well for several decades. Probably no other society has developed a more efficient system of education than has America during the past three-quarters of a century. Considering the circumstances of the times, the effectiveness of past education practices in our society was not reduced by the fact that the belief in fixed intelligence could not be verified by careful research. As long as it was believed that intelligence was of this sort and individuals acted on this belief, it made no difference whether it was verifiable or not.

ALTERNATE THEORIES OF INTELLIGENCE

The needs of our society have changed considerably, however, and society and science have brought us to the stage where the concept of fixed intelligence is no longer functional. In fact, it may be harmful. The belief in fixed and limited ability has not provided a fertile ground for the development of alternate theories of ability during the past decades. Although many psychologists have been concerned with research in learning, they have generally avoided the question of fixed intelligence and concentrated their efforts on the problems of learning which could be managed in the laboratory and other controlled situations. Most scientists in psychology have operated in a non-school context and have not given much attention to the practice of teaching and learning in the schools, and those who have generally ignored, until quite recently, alternate theories of learning. Educators have, therefore, found the contributions of psychologists difficult to adapt to the classroom.

During the period from 1930 to 1950, sociologists similarly avoided concern with education. Few sociologists or social psychologists were interested in research on the school and the educational processes. Although the fixed intelligence concept was not compatible with most sociological theories of socialization and the sociological emphasis on learning, sociologists have also generally accepted the notion of fixed abilities when operating as educators. Sociologists often use intelligence tests and other screening devices in the same way that public school educators do with little apparent knowledge of their reliability or validity.

Perhaps a new social psychology of learning with an emphasis on the interaction of the individual with his social environment will emerge to supplant the outmoded conception of fixed abilities. The developmental theories of Piaget[10] and the social reinforcement theories exemplified by Bandura and Walters[11] are being applied to the educational arena. Although there are varying interpretations of these and other theories, they suggest the possibility of a developmental process in the mental growth of the individual. In a similar fashion, many sociologists have recently become interested in various aspects of the educational system. Where formerly few were concerned with the field, now an extensive segment of sociologists is concentrating on various aspects of school organization and the educational processes. The new era among sociologists may have been signalled by Robert Faris' 1961 Presidential Address to the Sociological Association, which focused on the ability dimension in human society.[12] Faris pointed out that we are no longer bound by the conception of fixed abilities and that society essentially creates its own level of human abilities.

[10] There is a very extensive literature by J. Piaget and his associates which cannot all be cited here. Many sources provide this bibliography including Hunt, *op. cit.*

[11] Albert Bandura and Richard Walters, *Social Learning and Personality Development* (New York: Holt, Rinehart and Winston, 1967).

[12] Robert Faris, "The Ability Dimension in Human Society," *American Sociological Review* (December 1961), 26:835-42.

The theory of human behavior which guides the analysis in this book is similar to that expressed by Faris and other sociologists and social psychologists. It varies greatly from the traditional beliefs in fixed and limited abilities which have guided much educational practice.

A Social Psychological Conception of Learning

Our conception of learning is based on the observation that children learn to behave in the ways that the people with whom they associate behave. Although minor exceptions to this generalization can be found, the overpowering evidence demonstrates that children in every society learn to act, talk, and think much as their associates do. From this and related evidence we have derived several interrelated propositions which outline our general conception of learning.[13]

Basic components of every society or social group are the norms of behavior which characterize the group and its members. Thus *the social norms and expectations of others define the appropriate behavior for persons in various social situations.* Some of the norms or expectations may apply to all members of a given group but others may apply only to persons occupying certain positions. In either instance, boundaries of appropriate or proper behavior are defined by the social norms and expectations of others. *Each person learns the definitions of appropriate behavior through interaction with others who are important or significant to him.* With rare exceptions persons in every social unit acquire a conception of what is considered desirable and appropriate behavior in the various situations.

We postulate that through interaction with others *the individual learns to behave in the ways that he perceives are appropriate or proper for him.* Also, through interaction with certain others among his associates, the individual develops

---

[13] Much of this has been previously stated in W. B. Brookover, "A Social-Psychological Conception of Learning," *School and Society,* 87:84-87 (1959), and in W. B. Brookover and David Gottlieb, *A Sociology of Education,* 2nd Ed. (American Book Co. 1964), Chapter 1.

conceptions of what he ought to learn in varying social situations. Furthermore, and particularly relevant to the educational process, the *individual also acquires conceptions of his ability to learn various types of behavior through interaction with others whose evaluations are important to him.* This *self-concept of ability* is a necessary but not sufficient factor in determining the behavior he will learn. If the individual perceives that he is unable to learn certain types of behavior, this self-concept of ability will limit his learning of such behavior. The student who believes he does not have the ability to learn mathematics is not likely to do so. It is hypothesized that the individual will not attempt to learn those types of behavior which he perceives he is unable to learn. The self-concept of ability to learn does not, however, determine what the individual will learn. He may perceive that he is able to learn many types of behavior which are either inappropriate or improper for him to learn or he may perceive an alternate pattern of behavior among several from which he may choose.

In summary, a considerable proportion of what a student learns is dependent on his decisions to learn. These decisions are dependent on his conceptions of what is appropriate for self and what he thinks he is able to learn. In turn, the student's conceptions of self are acquired in interaction with others in his social systems.

These propositions project a social-psychological framework for the analysis of the educational process by emphasizing the importance of the social environment in which the student lives and his interaction with others in his social world. Such a conception of human learning has been identified as a *social interaction theory* because the individual acquires both the perceptions of appropriate behavior and his ability to learn in interaction with others who are important or significant to him. Not all members of groups or a society are equally significant. For each of us, certain persons and groups influence our perceptions of ourselves and our world more than others. We refer to these as *significant others* and *reference groups.* Interaction with reference groups and significant others account for much of the variation in student performances.

If these propositions are valid, the variations in individual behavior which occur between societies and within societies and groups may be explained in terms of the variations in the social-cultural environment. Although we recognize that there may be limits to the range of human learning that are fixed in the organism, we see no evidence that these are functional or that they have been identified except in a small number of individuals with specific organic defects. Too few people ever achieve up to their limits; they can always learn more. Functional limitations on learning, however, are imposed on each of us by our perceptions of what we are capable of and what we ought to be doing. With rare exceptions, the ability of human beings to learn is limited only by the social-cultural environments in which they live. They learn whatever the society defines as appropriate and provides for them to learn.

SUGGESTED READINGS

BOYER, WILLIAM H. and PAUL WALSH, "Are Children Born Equal?" *Saturday Review*, (Oct. 19, 1968), pp. 61 ff.

BROOKOVER, WILBUR B., EDSEL L. ERICKSON, and LEE M. JOINER. *Self-Concept and School Achievement Vol. III*, East Lansing, Michigan: Educational Publications Services, Michigan State University, 1967. A detailed presentation of the theory and research relevant to the development and effects of self-concept of ability.

FARIS, ROBERT, "The Ability Dimension in Human Society," *American Sociological Review* 26 (December 1961), pp. 835-842. Major points of this article are that societies create their own intellectual ability levels and that the belief in fixed human abilities is impeding our cultural development.

HUNT, J. McVICKER, *Intelligence and Experience*. New York: The Ronald Press Co., 1961. Chapters I, II and III. A comprehensive history of the nature-nurture controversy and intelligence testing.

ROSENTHAL, ROBERT and LENORE JACOBSON, *Pygmalion in the Classroom*. New York: Holt, Rinehart and Winston, Inc., 1968. This provocative study attempts to determine if the intellectual growth of children is related to the expectancies for such growth held by teachers. For a critical review see "On the Psychology of Expectation in the Classroom," Peter and Carol Gumpert, *The Urban Review*, Vol. 3, 1 (Sept. 1968), pp. 21-26.

2

Society
Culture
and
Education

IN ORDER TO SURVIVE, every society must be composed of persons who both share much common behavior and perform many diverse activities. Failure to teach either the common aspects of behavior or the necessary variety of behavior to new members could only result in disintegration. Every society must have a system of teaching all its new members certain common behavior as well as a system of allocating and training them for various specific activities.

Each society defines what all of its individuals should learn and what is appropriate for only certain individuals. Those patterns of behavior which are required or expected of all people in a given society or cultural group are known as *universals*.[1] These patterns of behavior can be readily identified in any given society. For example, with rare exceptions, all Americans learn to speak some variety of English, to wear clothes, and to eat certain types of food.

[1] Ralph Linton, *The Study of Man* (New York: D. Appleton Century Co., 1936).

Within every society there are also some areas of behavior within which *alternate patterns* are provided. In large, complex, and somewhat divergent societies such as the United States, the range of permissive alternates is somewhat greater than in a small, homogeneous society. In the United States, although wearing clothes is essentially universal in public situations, there are many ways in which clothes may be worn and many variations in type of clothes that are permissible. Thus, there are alternate patterns of clothes-wearing behavior from which the individual may choose or which he may be taught in various social groups. In school, some may learn a second language and others may not or some may learn algebra and others may not. These are alternate patterns of behavior which are selected by the individual or the school officials for the individual.

In addition to the universals and alternate patterns, Linton identified those types of behavior which are specific to particular members of the society as *specialties*. These are patterns of behavior that are expected of individuals occupying particular roles or statuses in the social system. Certain kinds of behavior are prescribed for females and other kinds of behavior are prescribed for males. In a similar fashion, teachers or doctors or farmers are expected to learn certain types of behavior that are defined as appropriate and proper for persons occupying those positions. Much formal education, at the higher levels particularly, is concerned with teaching the appropriate behavior for various specialties.

Every society provides some means of teaching all three types of behavior—universals, alternatives, and specialties—to new members of the society. Thus, there are both common education programs for all and differentiated education for various groups and individuals, with a system of assigning persons to the differentiated ones.

SOCIETY AND CULTURE

A traveler moving from one country to another is usually impressed by both similarities and differences among people in various areas. Certain types of behavior may be found in each society. Human beings all walk upright, speak a language, have some system of family relationships and means of producing and distributing food. At the same time, however, we are impressed by the differences between the behavior of people in one society and those in another. The language spoken, type of dress, religious beliefs, relations between male and female, and methods of production vary drastically in different parts of the world. These differences are so great that the inexperienced traveler may experience what is commonly known as "cultural shock." This phenomenon arises from the feelings of strangeness when we are surrounded by human beings, but we are unable to understand or comprehend the meaning and significance of the behavior which we observe. A state of panic may develop if we cannot relate to the people around us.

Among the more obvious and, perhaps, more crucial differences between people is the difference in their language. The inability to communicate through language presents a major barrier to understanding and knowledge of different peoples. A common language is one of the major bonds which relate the people of a particular society to one another and identify the boundaries of the society.

The common language suggests a third and perhaps most important observation about the peoples of the world. All the people in a particular society have some behaviors in common. Although there may be minor differences, the people in a given society speak the same language, dress essentially alike, eat similar food, have common beliefs and values, and behave alike in many other respects.

The differences between groups and the commonality within groups are apparently all learned, for we can observe that children moved from one society to another learn to speak and act like those about them. These similarities of behavior within a given group and differences between groups are characteristics of what social scientists term "culture." Cultures are always identified with particular societies so that we may define *a society* as *an organized group of individuals* and *a culture* as *an organized group of learned responses characteristic of a particular society.* We emphasize that culture is *learned* behavior associated with a particular society because teaching and learning the culture is the essence of education in any society.

The analysis of the processes by which culture is learned is therefore basic to our understanding of education. The very existence and persistence of any society is dependent on the learning of those patterns of behavior which are characteristic of its culture.

We can make two observations concerning the nature of culture and society and see their significance for analysis of the educability of human beings.

1. Human beings learn to behave in many different ways. There is not a single language but scores of languages characteristic of various societies around the world. There are widely differing patterns of behavior in almost any aspect of human life—religion, values, relations of men and women, dress, eating, and sleeping. Human organisms apparently have the ability to learn a very wide range of behavior—whatever is appropriate in their society.

2. Nearly all members of each society learn certain behavior patterns commonly expected in the society; Americans often discuss the difficulty of learning a foreign language and the relative complexity of various languages. In this we imply that some people cannot learn some languages, but with very rare exceptions, every child in any society learns whatever language is provided and deemed appropriate and proper for him to learn regardless of its complexity. American schools generally provide foreign language instruction for only those students with presumably high language ability, in spite of the fact that even rather retarded French children learn to speak French. The same, of course, could be said for all aspects of the common cultural behaviors. Walking, food consumption, dress, religion, and a complex pattern of relationships between sexes in each group, as well as many other aspects of the culture, are acquired by essentially all members of the society. This is such a universal phenomenon in every society including

our own that no question is ever raised concerning the possibility that a newborn child will fail to acquire the appropriate
patterns of human behavior. Of course a small proportion of
physical defectives do not learn to walk or talk, but the proportion is so small that the general expectation is that every
member in a society will acquire such appropriate behavior.
And more important, almost 100 per cent of the children do
learn such behavior.

Basic Aspects of Culture

Although the particular ways of doing so vary greatly,
every society must have some provision for meeting basic
needs of its members and maintaining itself. Children therefore must be taught these common patterns of behavior, and
the members of the society must behave in the appropriate
ways in these areas. A major function of any educational
system, both in and out of schools, is to teach these essential
and common modes of behaviors in the society. In order to
understand this primary educational function, we shall briefly
examine the types of behavior essential to the survival of any
society.[2]

The survival and maintenance of a society depends on the
process of teaching or transmitting the essential patterns of
behavior to its new members. Thus all children must be so-
cialized or educated to behave in a manner appropriate to
their society. No society could survive without universal knowledge of those patterns of behavior which provide the common
modes of operation in the society. Although the particular
types of behavior will vary greatly, all cultures must have some
common categories of behavior which are essential for its con-
tinuation.

► *System of Communication.* Common among all cultures or
all learned human behaviors is a complex of communication

[2] For an elaboration of the basic aspects of culture *see* Ralph Linton,
The Tree of Culture (New York: Alfred Knopf Co., 1955).

and interaction media of which language is the major component. Although there are vast differences in the nature of the language acquired, the members of every society learn the language which the older members of that society use. A system of communication is fundamental for the maintenance of any society. It is an essential medium by which other elements of the culture are transmitted from one group or individual to another and from one generation to another. Language provides the means by which the experience of the past is preserved.

► *Physical Survival.* The culture must be concerned with the patterns of behavior necessary to provide food, shelter, and other materials for physical survival. Every society has some patterns of behavior, although varying greatly from one to another, which provide the members of the society with physical nourishment, protection, and related needs. Without these, the society would disappear.

► *Community Living.* Techniques for living together in harmony and for the operation of essential common activities are an integral part of what we commonly identify as a society, but the various values and behavior patterns associated with living together in a particular social situation are an essential aspect of learned behavior. The techniques for living together involve many different forms, but certainly include patterns of sex and family relationships, patterns of association between generations, as well as some system of division of labor and assignment of various roles in the society.

► *Reproduction and Training.* The techniques of living together, of course, are closely associated with the patterns of reproduction and the training or education of the new generation. The survival of the society is dependent on the replacement of current members with new members of the society and the socialization of those in the appropriate and expected patterns of behavior in various situations. The system of sex relations, therefore, and the patterns of training or educating the young are essential to any culture.

► *System of Control.* Although the society succeeds in educating nearly all new members, it must also provide some means to control those members who are not adequately trained. In some societies the system of control is also associated with the patterns of behavior involved in eliminating some members from the society. This may involve execution or it may simply involve some system of ostracism or incarceration which removes an undesirable individual from the ongoing patterns of behavior in the society.

► *Recreation.* Every society must find a means of escape from the monotony and boredom of repeated behavior. Every culture, therefore, provides some kind of recreation or relief from the continous and routine activities which are otherwise essential for survival. These may take the form of games, storytelling, artistic activities, and a variety of other methods of release from the other essential aspects of the culture.

► *Reassurance.* The society must provide explanation and reassurance in periods of crisis. We generally identify such explanations as religion or magic. These patterns usually are associated with explanations of the nature of the universe and the belief system concerned with the origins of the culture and the society. Thus, the reassurance in times of crisis and the satisfaction of general curiosity of the members concerning the society and the world in which they live are generally associated in a complex of beliefs and explanations.

Although we frequently associate our basic beliefs with religion, it should be recognized that all common aspects of culture involve strongly held values and beliefs which are taught to the new generations from birth. Thus, the value attached to certain kinds of food and beliefs about the danger of other materials that might be used for foodstuffs are strongly held, and the value of behavior associated with food as well as all of the other essential aspects of the culture are basic to the survival of a given society. The system of beliefs which perpetuates the valued behavior is therefore also an essential part of the total cultural system.

This classification of the types of behavior that all members of the society must acquire does not include all of the culture which is taught. In addition to the common aspects of culture, every society must provide means for teaching particular members of the society to function in different roles. Most obvious of these, of course, are the differences in male and female behavior in every society. In addition to the division of labor between the sexes, there are many specialized functions in a particular society which must be provided. The extent of this division of labor and its degree of specialization varies greatly from one society to another. In smaller societies the degree of specialization and division of labor is relatively slight. Most men in such societies will perform similar functions and women will participate in other activities. A few, however, will be taught special roles such as those of medicine man or midwife. In larger societies which have a higher degree of division of labor there are many different specializations which must be acquired by some members. Each society, in order to survive, must develop means of teaching or transmitting to new members both the common culture and the more specialized patterns of behavior.

THE TRANSMISSION OF CULTURE

The methods by which the culture is transmitted or taught to the new members of the society vary from one society to another. These methods may be identified in two general categories: the informal methods which are continuous patterns of teaching in the society and the formal methods which involve the organization of special institutions or agencies to do the teaching. In the former, all members of the society are learners or recipients of the culture and all members are also teachers or givers of the culture. Every member of the society who has acquired any of the common patterns of behavior in time becomes a model to be observed by others. Each individual also communicates to those with whom he interacts what he perceives is the appropriate and proper behavior for each situation in which they interact. The teaching and learning of many aspects of the culture is, therefore, a continuous process in society. The formal socialization or education processes involve the designation of particular agents of the culture to teach the younger members of the society. Although common aspects of the culture are taught in these formally organized institutions, which we call schools, a considerable portion of the function of these institutions is to teach the more specialized roles and some patterns of behavior that are not required of all people.

In societies with relatively homogeneous patterns of economic activity, the educational process within which the cultural behavior is learned is entirely or almost entirely informal. By that we mean there are few if any specified teachers of the culture. A few people may be designated to teach a limited number of some specialist activities, but most of the cultural behavior is acquired within the on-going day-to-day activities which are not specified as education. In the larger and more diversified societies such as our own, the proportion of the teaching delegated to special teachers is somewhat larger. It must be recognized, however, that most of the common learnings such as language, food, shelter, dress, behavior, as well as fundamental beliefs associated with the society, are largely acquired without a formal institutionalized school program. The formal school program supplements other activities in teaching the common cultural patterns, but it does not assume the major responsibility for them.

The formal educational institutions in our society teach special skills of reading and a number system as well as other knowledge which are the means by which one may acquire additional cultural knowledge. This is particularly essential in extensive and elaborate cultural systems found in the highly developed societies. Much of the accumulated experience or culture is stored in written language or by other means. Much of the accumulated knowledge is essential for performing certain tasks in the society and in developing new knowledge. Thus, in contrast to the non-literate societies, much of the accumulated culture is transmitted by written and related media. The schools in our society have been assigned major responsibility for teaching the skills which are necessary for learning this accumulated culture or any portion of it.

In the more homogeneous hunting or fishing or agricultural societies, a relatively narrow range of economic activities was necessary and nearly everyone learned the essential behaviors connected with the production of food, shelter, and other human needs in the informal process of socialization. In the more heterogeneous societies with their vast complex of specializations and division of labor, the new members of the society were unable to interact with all specialties and the process of acquiring particular specialized vocational knowledge has been assigned to formal educational systems. The doctors, lawyers, and school teachers, as well as many other professionals, are educated by formal schooling.

Even in the formal educational setting, however, a major portion of the behavior is learned through the informal relationships with other learners as well as teachers. In the informal educational process, of course, the older people take on many characteristics of the specialized teacher role. The distinction between the formal and informal education is not, therefore, as sharp as one might believe. In both, the process is essentially one of social interaction between the teacher and the learner. The educational process is, therefore, in essence, a social process. Some understanding of the formal processes of education may, therefore, be acquired through an analysis of the more general informal process of socialization.

The Process of Cultural Learning

In our observations about society and culture, we noted first that behavior in two societies differs significantly; yet at the same time, within a given society essentially all members of the society learn the common patterns of behavior, such as language, dress, patterns of relations between members of the family. This latter observation raises a very significant question for education: What makes the process of teaching and learning the common cultural behavior so universally successful? Observation of the differences in cultural behavior makes it quite clear that new members of society must learn the common patterns of behavior. These behaviors are not fixed in the organism because the newborn child acquires whatever language and other patterns of behavior are common to the people with whom he associates. Although we have not commonly identified this process as an educational one, its universal effectiveness suggests that we could learn much from an understanding of the processes of teaching and learning in the informal patterns of socialization. We shall analyze this process and compare informal social learning with the formal educational process in American schools. Below are characteristics of the socialization process.

1. All *people are teachers.* No specifically identified persons are the exclusive teachers of any particular behavior. All adults who associate with the child help to teach him the culturally expected behavior. All the members of the society are models and constantly teach the language and other common aspects of the culture. All members of the society are learners of the culture and all members are also teachers. The parents and older members of the family system may be expected to assume a greater responsibility for teaching certain aspects of the culture than other members of the society, but no one person or group of persons is specifically identified as the teacher of the language, food habits, dress patterns, or any other commonly acquired patterns of behavior. Since the members of the family group are in more continuous contact with the new member, they are more likely to be the significant teachers of the appropriate behavior. All are teachers in the sense that they contribute to the process of transmitting the appropriate patterns of behavior to the child and none avoid this process by suggesting that it is the responsibility of a special teacher.

2. *Universality of expectations.* All people are expected to learn certain aspects of the culture. The common expectations are universally applied *to* all members of the society *by* all members of the society. In relatively small societies where the division of labor is limited, the same practice may characterize the teaching of certain specialties. In these instances a single individual may be allocated to a particular role, but everyone in the society expects that particular individual to learn the role. Thus a specific member of the society is identified as the future medicine man and everyone expects that individual to learn the medicine man behavior. Thus, in special ascribed roles as well as the universals of the culture, there may be a common or universal set of expectations which applies to certain members of the society. In either case, everyone agrees on the kinds of behavior all children ought to learn.

3. *Homogeneity of models.* All members of the family, neighborhood, and other associates speak the same language, dress in similar manner, eat food in the same ways, and behave in many other similar ways. The child is therefore not presented a variety of models from which he must select the common human behavior patterns. Of course, there are differences in the models for male and female and other status differences, but these differences are clearly defined and the newborn child is taught very early in life which is the appropriate model for him or her. All members of the society behave within the culturally defined range of behavior for persons of their particular type, and the child does not interact with persons who behave outside the range of appropriateness except in rare instances. In the cases where association with non-approved models does occur, this is clearly defined and communicated to the child.

4. *Continuous nature of teaching.* The child in any society is dependent on the association with and care of other members of the society. He is therefore in continuous interaction with other members of the society who function as teachers of the common patterns of behavior. Thus, he interacts regularly and continuously with walking human beings and talkers

of a particular language. The teaching of these patterns of behavior is not set aside for a particular time with particularly formalized methods of communicating them. The teaching is available throughout the waking hours and in all the child's associations. The learning of a language is in this context decidedly different from the process by which we commonly attempt to teach a language in school. In the latter case, only one or at most a few people work at the teaching of the language and this for only short periods of time periodically through the day or week. Our attempts to teach the "correct" language of the educated to children who have learned a colloquial version of the language in their family is a decidedly different process. A periodic attempt to teach a child such correct "teacher" English when he is constantly using and being taught by other associations a colloquial version of English is not likely to be significantly successful. If, however, the child were to associate on a continuous basis only with people who spoke the "correct" language, it is quite clear that he would acquire this form of language.

5. *Consistent and repeated use of approval and disapproval or reward and punishment for appropriate and expected behavior.* The child associates only with people who hold common expectations and behave in the common manner. He is consistently and repeatedly disapproved for behaving in any inappropriate manner. The approval and disapproval frequently takes the form of specific rewards or punishment when the behavior exhibited by the child goes beyond the accepted boundaries of required and expected behavior.

This continuous and consistent pattern of approval and disapproval contrasts markedly with the way academic subjects are taught in our schools. When a child behaves inappropriately in school, such as misspelling a word, it is not uncommon for the teacher and others to be inconsistent in their responses to the student. Thus the child may in some arenas of interaction be approved for failure or not learning "correct" language and certainly is not consistently disapproved or punished for speaking the public language that differs from the formal teacher language. Many other patterns of behavior such as knowledge and understanding of history or the manifestation of skill in the use of numbers and algebraic formulations are not the subject of consistent and repeated approval; neither is the failure to behave in these areas the object of consistent and repeated disapproval and/or punishment. Girls who may not be able to learn mathematics may be able to learn rather complex and abstract patterns of female behavior and complicated methods of relating to the opposite sex.

In spite of great differences among societies in the demands imposed on their members, essentially all children in each social system acquire the commonly demanded behaviors of the social systems in which they participate. Regardless of any presumed differences in biological organism or other factors which might affect ability to learn, all children except the clearly identified defectives do acquire the common patterns of behavior. The particular time at which specific behavior patterns may be mastered varies somewhat among children, but the fact remains that all learn the language and all learn to eat the appropriate food.

Some types of behavior are universally acquired in a similar fashion in the typical school situation. Dress styles and language variations occur between schools in different communities. We are frequently able to identify students in a given school by the particular variations in dress. Other norms of behavior can be identified for various school groups. In these instances, essentially all members of the group acquire the expected patterns of behavior. Thus the co-eds in a particular high school or college will tend not only to wear the same kinds of clothing, but wear them in much the same manner.

The effectiveness of the informal socialization process in non-academic types of behavior leads us to hypothesize that academic behaviors would be learned in the same manner if similar patterns of expectation and processes of teaching were employed. Perhaps algebra behavior would be as universally and effectively learned as the colloquial language is in every society if the same processes of socialization were applied to algebra as are to the local language.

In contrast to the process which characterizes the non-academic socialization process, we build our formal education program on a model that assumes that only a portion of the people can or will learn certain kinds of behavior. This assumption then is related to our practice with regard to teaching various types of academic behavior. We not only do not provide universal expectations that a child will learn various types of academic subject matter such as algebra or history or science, but we provide a range of heterogeneous models which communicate to the child that many persons do not and perhaps should not learn the behavior which is taught in a particular classroom.

The heterogeneity of models is, of course, associated with discontinuity of teaching and vast differences in patterns of approval and disapproval with regard to the behavior involved. Thus, it is common for both teachers and parents, as well as other associates, to communicate to most girls and some boys that the learning of algebra is not expected and to provide approval for non-learning of algebra behavior. Thus, many students are rewarded and taught *not* to learn particular kinds of behavior which the school is designed to teach other students. It is not surprising therefore that the teaching of algebra behavior or formal grammar is not universally effective in American schools. In fact the norms of the system would be grossly violated if all children learned the same or similar amounts of subject matter in a given period of time. It seems likely that the process of socializing individuals in a given society would fail to a similar extent if the members of the society assumed that only a few could learn to be Americans or Chinese and if the methods teaching culturally required behavior was designed as our educational system is. If we identified specific teachers of the language and other common cultural behavior, the individual associated with people who behaved in other ways as well as with the teachers of the culture, and was given support or approval for not behaving in

the culturally expected manner, it is likely that the effectiveness of the non-school socialization process would be drastically
reduced.

Common vs. Differentiated
Socialization

In complex societies, particularly, every individual must
learn both the common cultural patterns and a variety of differentiated roles, if the society is to function adequately. Both
informal and formal processes of socialization must, therefore,
function to teach common patterns of behavior to all people
and particular functions to selected individuals. The latter re-
quires that there be some provision for the identification and
selection of persons who receive particular kinds of education.
Although the informal socialization system in our society con-
tributes to both aspects of the process—common and differentiated—the dual functions are characteristic of formal
education in the United States and other industrialized nations.

Although some aspects of the formal schooling program
are presumed to be common or universal in the society, many
parts of the behavior taught in formal educational systems are
identified as alternative modes of behaving. The concept of
common school derived from the notion that there were certain kinds of behavior that all children should acquire in
common. These, of course, included a minimum level of a
common language usage—speaking, reading, and writing—
and some use of arithmetic skills. The school also reinforced
and supplemented the teaching of common beliefs and other
patterns of expected behavior in the common program.

The diverse cultural backgrounds from which the American population came and the relatively limited range of occupations requiring specialized skills gave priority to the common
school program during the nineteenth century in the United
States. In order to provide a common cultural base for the
development of a society, the American schools taught many
immigrant children to speak English and used English as the
medium of instruction for all aspects of the curriculum. The

basic beliefs and values of the new society were the primary focus of much of the material which children learned to read. Since only a few people with specialized occupational skills were needed, only a few students were educated beyond the common elementary school during this period. For several decades, therefore, the common school program was the predominant emphasis in America education.

The rapid industrialization and emphasis on differentiated needs of individual children in recent decades has drastically reduced the emphasis on common education. As secondary education expanded, we developed differentiated educational programs to prepare students for different occupations and positions in society. The vocational education and other specialized curricula which developed a half-century ago are characteristic of this movement toward differentiated education at the secondary level. With the development of the differentiated secondary program we acquired the belief in individual differences in ability to learn and introduced the practice of measuring the differences. This combination of forces provided the basis for extending the differentiated or individualized curriculum into the elementary school. The emphasis on differentiated programs for individuals has overshadowed the common elements in American education. But the transmission of the culturally defined beliefs, values, language, and other behavior expected of all members of the society remains an essential function of formal education as well as of the informal socialization process.

Differentiated socialization to prepare persons for various statuses or positions in the society involves the educational system in several crucial social decisions. How much common or general education is necessary for all? At what stage should differentiated education be initiated? On what basis should persons be selected for differentiated education? Who should select the students for specific types of education? Much of the discussion in this book relates to these questions. We have already noted in Chapter 1 that the theory of abilities or educability prevalent in the educational system affects the way the questions are answered. The traditional belief in relatively fixed abilities has been a primary basis for the differentiated educational selection. The belief that the educators could identify such abilities and the extended periods of school attendance in high schools and colleges have resulted in the educational system assuming a major role in the allocation of persons to various positions in society.

Educational Allocation

Until recent decades, most vocations were filled by men without formal education. Our history is filled with examples of bank presidents and corporation executives who emerged from on-the-job experiences with little formal education. Today, few major banks would consider hiring anyone even at the lowest junior office position who did not have a college degree. Today, nearly all jobs with large employers require some formal education.

As our society has become more and more technologically complex, with greater and greater vocational specialization, formal educational credentials have become more and more the keys by which individuals attain occupational opportunities. Sometimes the requirements are specific vocational credentials such as a Doctor of Medicine degree. Sometimes the requirements are general status credentials such as a high-school diploma or a college degree. At any rate, whether they are specific vocational credentials such as "certified teacher" or general status credentials, more and more the authority to grant these credentials is vested in our formally sanctioned educational institutions. Medical schools hold the responsibility of determining who will be eligible to take state medical examinations to qualify to practice medicine.

In a less obvious way, the high schools and elementary schools also determine who will and who will not be eligible to be a banker, doctor, engineer. When a high school places a student in a special education program, a non-college preparatory program, or a slow track program, it is actually impeding the student's entry into some occupations and encouraging his entry into others.

In essence, each level of education provides the credentials for the next level of education until the credentials are sufficient for occupational entry. In other words, the sorting and selecting of students for varying educational programs, along with formal educational prerequisites for occupational entry, gives to the school one of its most important functions— the "allocation function."

This process of identification and selection for different occupations and positions in society begins early in the school career of the child. Various decisions and evaluations are made about children in the early elementary grades and continue throughout their academic careers. The accumulation of evaluations made of students and decisions which are made about students largely determine both the kind and the amount of formal education which the child is likely to receive and his participation in society. By the time the student reaches the senior high school, he has been generally identified as a learner of academic subjects or a learner of non-academic subjects. In this process he becomes identified as a "college-bound" or a "non-college-bound" student. In many high schools there are three or four "tracks." In any case, educators control the destinies of their charges by what they teach or do not teach them. They also control who gets certain occupational chances and who does not, often on the basis of assumed intellectual capacities assessed by intelligence and other tests.

The allocation function of assigning students to varying occupational opportunities influences not only what the students learn but also their abilities to learn. This function of allocating certain individuals to certain programs influences the learning of students by structuring how others will react to each student as well as how each student will react to himself.

The "gate-keeper" role of education developed as American society became industrialized and a high degree of occupational specialization occurred. It seemed necessary to develop a system for allocating people to different kinds of positions. In the absence of other means, the educational system became the primary agency for selecting and allocating people to different positions in the society. Thus the level of education and the type of education received is an essential factor in the placement or allocation of individuals in various positions. During the past decades when large proportions of Americans were needed in unskilled and semi-skilled occupations, a proportion of the students in school were provided a minimum level of common education and identified as non-learners of the "more advanced" levels of education. The relatively small proportion needed for professional and high levels of technical skill was selected on the basis of its assignment to academic kinds of education in the elementary and secondary schools.

This system of alternate educational programs and the associated allocation to various positions and statuses in society has functioned extremely well in the United States until recently. Through the development of a belief system that these people have varied, fixed, and limited abilities and that a testing and counseling program can allocate people with presumably different kinds and levels of ability to differing educational programs, the educational system has provided workers with varying levels and types of education for a wide range of occupations and related positions in society.

The current concern with the education of the disadvantaged arises from a change in the American labor force which no longer provides opportunity for a high proportion of unskilled and semi-skilled workers with low levels of general education and an unfilled demand to fill vacant higher level occupational roles. There are many contemporary efforts, therefore, to increase the proportion of students and children who will be taught the higher levels of academic subjects. Our schools are adequately tooled according to the beliefs that predominate in them to serve the needs of the older rural America. Whether the schools can be altered by new beliefs to meet the demands of the emerging America, with its demands for an ever-increasing proportion of citizens with higher academic skills, is open to question.

SUGGESTED READINGS

BROOKOVER, WILBUR B. and DAVID GOTTLIEB, *A Sociology of Education*. New York: American Book Company, 1964, Chapter III. Examined are the expectations Americans hold for education along with the manifest and latent functions of education in an industrialized society.

KNELLER, GEORGE F. *Educational Anthropology*. New York: John Wiley and Sons, Inc., 1965. An easily read introduction to the anthropological study of education which examines the assumptions of anthropologists as well as the practices of education.

THUT, I. N. and DON ADAMS. *Educational Patterns in Contemporary Societies*. New York: McGraw-Hill, 1964. This text will acquaint the reader with the major patterns of educational systems in the world in relation to their national and cultural settings.

3

Sub-Cultural
Variation
and
Education

WHILE ALL MEMBERS of a society share a common culture, each will be unique to the extent that his sub-cultural experience will vary from the sub-cultural experiences of others. In the United States, we may identify several sub-societies and accompanying sub-cultures which differ in varying degrees in language, religious beliefs, economic activities, or other patterns of behavior. Educational policies are frequently related to such sub-cultural differences and the variations in behavior learned outside of school may affect school achievement. A knowledge of sub-cultural variations is therefore essential to understand the American educational system and the achievement of its students.

Among the more important of the sub-society or sub-cultural variations in the United States are those related to geographical region, rural and urban locale, ethnic affiliation, racial identity, and socio-economic status level. Important variations also occur between various other categories of people. The behavior of the adolescent age-group varies significantly from that of people over forty, and young first year teachers differ from the veterans of many years of teaching. In similar fashion, groups within a school vary in their values, norms, and behavioral patterns. These take on some characteristics of sub-cultures or sub-societies. The line dividing sub-cultures from groups is often difficult to make. We will defer further discussion of variations in adolescent sub-cultures or groups to Chapter 4. Our concern in this chapter is with the broad categories of sub-cultural variation which are related to education in the United States.

Before we examine these sub-cultural variations in greater detail, however, it is necessary to briefly consider the general impact of education on such sub-societies, and the reverse, the significance of sub-society for education. Here we shall examine the goals, policies, and practices of both education and the larger society.

SUB-CULTURAL GOALS OF EDUCATION

Paradoxically, in the United States we have sought to simultaneously maintain and reduce sub-cultural differences. In several areas, the goal of American society has been to reduce sub-cultural diversity as much and as rapidly as possible. Perhaps the most extensive program for the reduction of cultural differences was that through which immigrants from a wide range of European and Asiatic societies were molded to fit into a relatively common American culture. Throughout the latter decades of the nineteenth century and the first quarter of this century when immigration was extensive, the social policy of American society was to Americanize the immigrants as rapidly as possible. Although other forces participated in this process, a major agency in the acculturation of European and Asiatic immigrants was the educational system. Knowledge of the government and the ideals and beliefs which characterized America were essential parts of the Americanization process.

▶ *Goals for European Immigrants.* Throughout this period of Americanization of immigrant children, emphasis was placed on the use of English in the schools. With a few exceptions, English was the language in which American educational programs were carried on. In fact, the children of many immigrant families first learned English in school. The learning of English was strongly associated with the objective of Americanizing the new members of the society from diverse cultural backgrounds.

▶ *Canadian Goals.* In contrast to that of the United States, the policy in Quebec and some other parts of Canada has been to perpetuate the differences in the French-Canadian and English-Canadian sub-societies. The support of separate schools for French-Canadians and the maintenance of two languages in both schools and public exchange have served to maintain and to some extent aggravate the differences in the two sub-cultures.

▶ *Goals for American Indians.* There are recognizable instances in which a contrary policy with regard to cultural diversity has been followed with clearly different goals. Illustrative of goals which are contrary to a policy of acculturation into the mainstream of America, but little talked about in education circles, are those which directed the education of American Indians. There has been some vacillation with regard to the objectives and policies concerning the American Indian, but during the major portion of our history the government has sought to maintain the separate Indian cultures and to perpetuate the diversity. A major means of doing this was the organization and maintenance of separate Indian reservation schools. At various times and particularly in recent years, we have verbalized the desire to educate the American Indians so that they might become acculturated into the mainstreams of American life. However, the programs provided and the prevailing perceptions of the Indians as different and perhaps inferior[1] have had the effect of impeding acculturation and perpetuating the American Indian sub-societies.

► *Goals for Black Americans.* Although the goals are somewhat blurred, it seems that the segregation of Negroes in American schools and in society generally was at least partly designed to perpetuate separate and different sub-societies within the United States. Certainly, in many ways white Americans have sought to reduce the movement of black Americans across caste lines; the maintenance of segregated schools for Negroes has served to perpetuate the caste differentiation. We may safely conclude then that the maintenance of separate schools for American Indians and Negroes in our society has had a somewhat different set of goals and a different impact than did the schools provided for European immigrants where the emphasis was upon rapid acculturation. Even so, through the sharing of textbooks, curricula, and the English language, some common socialization has occurred in separate schools.

► *Goals for Rural and Urban Children.* The goals of American education with regard to the perpetuation of rural-urban differences have been less clearly defined and less consistent. There are, however, some vestiges of educational objectives to maintain rural "purity" in contrast to "city-slicker" ways. In spite of the extensive patterns of interaction between rural and urban people and the extensive urbanization of American society, many rural communities resist the consolidation of their schools with city districts. It is not unusual to find separate school districts serving rural areas which surround a city school district. In some instances the surrounding rural area is organized into a single district to circumvent a merger with the town or city. These local school organization patterns are not the result of pure chance. Although costs of education and related tax matters may be involved in the local school dis-

[1] Murray Wax, Rosalie Wax, and Robert J. Dumont, *Education in An American Indian Community,* Supplement to *Social Problems,* Vol. II, No. 4 (Spring 1964).

trict organization, the desire to maintain some separation is not irrelevant in many cases. Many rural people do not want their children to be exposed to what they perceive to be the undesirable aspects of city culture.

Similarly, many suburban areas insist on maintaining separate attendance areas and/or separate districts in order to avoid contamination with what they perceive as the inner-city sub-culture. This, of course, is an attempt to maintain the diversity and perpetuate the perceived qualities of the middle and upper classes which are concentrated in the suburban areas.

It seems clear from these examples that Americans have held ambivalent if not clearly conflicting goals with regard to the perpetuation or reduction of sub-cultural diversity. In some areas, Americans have sought to reduce the differences and have planned educational programs to serve this end. In other areas, however, Americans have followed exactly the opposite policy by maintaining, and in some cases increasing, the differences through the organization of separate school programs.

EDUCATIONAL POLICY AND CULTURAL DIVERSITY

► *Local vs. Centralized Control.* Educational policies and practices may also be the consequence of societal values not specifically directed toward education. Local control of the schools is a function of the political values placed on states' rights and local political control. The pressure of rural people in particular to maintain local control of their educational systems is derived from a desire to maintain the diversity and separation from the urban society. Resistance to federal influences is also related to the desire to maintain segregated school systems of other types. The maintenance of neighborhood school attendance areas and *de facto* segregated schools in suburban areas versus the central city is much more readily possible if the local agencies control educational policy and practice. Centralized control is more likely to be directed toward the reduction of diversity than is local control. There are exceptions to this generalization, however. For example, the federal operation of Indian education has tended to perpetuate the segregated Indian school system, while the operation of the Indian educational program by state and local agencies has in some cases resulted in integration of the Indian population with the dominant school groups. The process of Americanization and the teaching in English rather than in various other languages would probably have been less universal in its reduction of diversity among immigant children if there had not been some state control of the educational system.

▶ *Common vs. Specialized Education.* Policies concerning common versus diversified curricula are also related to the reduction or maintenance of cultural diversity. The concept of a "common"school which prevailed in most of the United States in the period in which mass education was developing emphasized the importance of giving a common experience to diverse groups of children. All children in the community regardless of differential ethnic origins and backgrounds were provided a common elementary school experience. This practice has continued to prevail to some extent in much of American education. Concomitant with the policy of general or common education, however, is the policy of providing varied curricula for different groups. The justification for such variation may be on a different basis but to a considerable extent at least the provision for different curricula serves to maintain sub-cultural differences. For example, the college preparatory curriculum may be provided primarily for middle or upper class students while the vocational or general curricula primarily serve lower class students. The consequence is to maintain differences between those in the lower socio-economic strata and those who are more affluent.

The system of school organizations may also be associated with the maintenance of sub-society variation. The separation of curriculum groups in different schools such as vocational or academic high schools may serve the same function as schools segregated on the basis of race or other social strata. The separation of a special educational program into a segregated group or building may serve to maintain sub-cultural differences. Although it may be unintended, any school system with differentiated programs and multiple buildings may be organized so that attendance and segregated school programs are related to sub-society differences. *Separate schools which serve varied sub-cultural groups generally do not reduce the diversity or increase mobility. Rather, they are likely to perpetuate, if not increase, the diversity.*

SUB-CULTURAL VARIATIONS IN THE UNITED STATES

It is likely that the variations in behavior among sub-societies have been decreasing over a number of decades. The Americanization of many diverse peoples among our migrants has been a national policy. The educational system, particularly "common" education, has provided a major arena within which the diversities among our immigrants have been reduced. The rapidly increasing ease of communication through mass media, as well as the mobility of the American population from one community to another and through the various segments of the society, also tends to reduce the differences. The educational system has provided the means for social mobility in the society and through this has further contributed to a reduction in the sub-society differences. However, in spite of the forces operating to minimize sub-cultural differences, we are able to identify variations among some strata and sub-societies in the United States.

Regional Variations

Although we cannot here identify all of the characteristics of the various regional cultures, it is generally recognized that the culture of certain geographic areas varies. The South particularly varies in a number of characteristics from other regions. We may identify also the New England states, the Great Plains area, Southwest, and other sub-cultural regions by differences in language accent, mobility, occupational and industrial distribution, political behavior, and religious beliefs. Although regional patterns of behavior may not produce major variation in formal education, they have some impact. The extent of outward migration in contrast to the maintenance of local identification may materially affect the type of occupational skills and orientation that the child is provided at the higher educational level. Language differences may be sufficient to cause some difficulty with written language and the use of instructional materials.[2]

Perhaps the most significant aspect of regional differences is found in those instances where other differences such as the level of income or the racial or ethnic characteristics coincide to some degree with regional areas. Thus, we identify contemporary Appalachia as a regional area which is also educationally and economically disadvantaged. Likewise, the differences in patterns of *de facto* segregation between the North and the South make significant differences in the educational organization and processes between these regional areas.

Rural-Urban Variations

The rural-urban behavior differences have declined more rapidly than those among other sub-society categories. The rapid decrease in the number of Americans engaged in agriculture and the increase in communication and mobility between rural and urban areas have greatly reduced the rural-urban behavior differences. In spite of the changes, however, some differences do remain in the rural farm segments of our society when compared to the urban.

One of the most important differences is the vocabulary and knowledge which the child acquires in the local urban or rural societies. The farm boys and girls learn an extensive vocabulary and knowledge of crops, farm animals, agricultural

---

[2] *See* Basil Bernstein, "Language and Social Class," *British Journal of Sociology*, 11:271-76 (1960).

equipment, soils, and related activities which may be completely unknown to the city child. Although the reverse difference is not as great because of the rural child's exposure to city culture, it is clear that city children learn different vocabulary and quite a different material culture. The differences in rural and urban cultures are also evident in educational and occupational aspirations. The rural youth has a more limited range. The differences in time schedule and the hours devoted to work, as well as the patterns of independence, also produce somewhat different beliefs and attitudes toward work.

The rural-urban cultural differences raise certain questions concerning the formal educational program. Rural boys and girls do less well on commonly used tests of academic aptitude than do the urban youth. Although differences in the quality of formal education may account in part for the lower performance of rural youth, the fact that the tests are largely based on urban cultural orientations and contain relatively little of the uniquely rural cultural learnings is probably the major reason for the difference in test performance. Tests of intelligence or aptitude seldom include vocabulary associated with farm animals, farm implements, the various kinds of agricultural crops, or related cultural phenomena. The vocabulary which the rural farm boy or girl acquires in these areas is of relatively little use in performance on the established educational measurements and related instruments. These differences are frequently translated by educators into differences in ability and modifications of the curriculum for children with rural backgrounds.

The development of the agricultural-oriented curriculum during the past forty years or so has served as an extremely valuable function in the education of farmers for improved agricultural production. This and other forces have increased production so rapidly that the need to provide agricultural education for rural youth has greatly declined. The small proportion of the population now engaged in agriculture produces much more food and fiber than was formerly produced by a majority of the population. Only a fraction of the farm youth can remain in agriculture. It is now necessary to educate a large proportion of rural students for migration to urban jobs.

Ethnic Variations

Most ethnic groups are now well assimilated into American society. Although we speak of Italian-Americans or Polish-Americans and occasionally German-Americans or Japanese-Americans, the third or fourth generation of children from these ethnic backgrounds are barely distinguishable from others. Except for a few groups, the differences among the descendants of immigrants are now so slight that they do not significantly affect the educational process.

In contrast with the major ethnic groups of an earlier day, some remnants of ethnic variation still exist and new ones have developed in recent years. In spite of the long history of their education, some American Indian groups remain divergent sub-cultures. As we have noted earlier, this, in part at least, results from the policy of maintaining separate schools and providing a differentiated educational program for the children of various Indian societies. This policy was based on the assumption that the differences required different schools or the desire of the dominant group to maintain the diverse culture.

The settlements of Amish and some other religious sects which continue to exist as divergent cultural islands do so in spite of the willingness and desire of dominant groups to assimilate them. The Amish, of course, are one of the more visible of these small divergent religious sects at the present time. Such groups maintain their sub-cultural diversity by isolating themselves from the mainstreams of American culture and setting rigid boundaries of appropriate behavior for their own society. The traditional Amish limitations on public school attendance and their insistence that schools must be taught by their own members are, of course, a part of the program designed to maintain a distinct sub-culture. American political and educational policy concerning the acculturation of the

Amish and similar groups has vacillated throughout our history. Although state education laws and related policies require that all schools be taught by certified teachers with specific patterns of training and that children remain in schools meeting specific standards to a minimum age, the Amish have generally been permitted to maintain their own schools which meet neither the legal nor the generally accepted standards of curriculum, school organization, or teacher qualification.

The largest contemporary ethnic sub-societies in America are the Spanish-speaking migrants from Puerto Rico, Mexico, and other areas. Large numbers of Puerto Ricans, Mexicans, and Cubans have moved to the continental United States in recent years. The implications for educational policy are evident. In general, for the Spanish-speaking groups the earlier policy of acculturation of immigrants has continued. Thus, the general function of the educational system is to assist in the assimilation of these groups in the culture of continental United States. Like those of the earlier immigrants from Europe, the differences in native language, of course, affect the readiness of the Spanish-speaking children to learn some types of behavior in our schools. The difference in pre-school socialization, including language, may also cause Spanish-speaking children to be identified as low-ability students.

Since many Mexican-Americans are migrant workers who move about in the United States, and since educational policy is governed largely by state and local units, the educational system has tended to assume little responsibility for the education of their children. The process of acculturation and assimilation may be somewhat retarded among such laborers. However, as America changes its policy with regard to the Spanish-speaking sub-societies, they are likely to assimilate in essentially the same manner as the European immigrants.

Racial Variations

Race is most accurately a biological classification based on a combination of physical traits and not a social or cultural phenomenon. As a biological classification it has little relevance for education, but the manner in which people respond to racial identification is of particular concern. In the United States and some other societies, racial identification is a basis on which much social interaction is structured. Although those identified as Negro in the United States have somewhat different biological characteristics from those identified as white, there are many exceptions to this. A significant number of people identified as white have features which would characterize them as negroid to a greater extent than many people who are identified as Negro. In the United States, identification as a Negro is often determined by membership in a social category rather than by physical traits. In this context many people identified as black, Afro-American, or Negro in the United States make up sub-societies with unique subcultured features.

In the past, and to a considerable extent still, the two racial groups operate as a caste system. Although interaction is common in certain areas of behavior, there are certain social situations such as intermarriage which have been generally opposed.

Since there has been considerable range of interaction and a very limited amount of passing from the Negro to white societies, the Negro-white caste system has had considerable overlap with the social class system in the United States. This is illustrated by the differential economic and educational levels of the two sub-societies. The occupations, income, and level of education of non-whites have and continue to be on the average lower than those of the whites. The majority of Negro people have jobs and incomes similar to those of the lower socio-economic strata of the white population. The educated Negroes who have been able to acquire higher status occupations have behavior similar to that of the middle-class whites. Although these similarities are great, and the racial sub-classifications must always be examined in relation to the criterion of social class identification, the social system in the United States does differentiate between persons identified as Negro and those identified as white. As we shall see in Chapter 6, this social system governing black-white relationships is undergoing, and will continue to undergo, fundamental change.

Socio-Economic Status Variations

An extensive literature on the stratification of American society has developed in recent years.[3] Although there are many diverse meanings and much discussion concerning the appropriate bases for delineating social class, there is general agreement that different strata can be identified in American society.

Various criteria have been used to differentiate class groups. The first criterion for identifying social class categories is the level of prestige in the community. The second criterion is the classification of people according to the power which they exert and hold in the community. The third criterion is a category of people with relatively similar behavior, sentiments, and interests which are distinguishable from those of another class. Considerable confusion arises if we attempt to conceptualize social class on one or the other or a combination of these criteria. Although these criteria are distinguishable in an abstract sense, they are not separate and distinct in the actual operation of the class system. Thus differences in prestige, power, and interests are almost always interrelated in a total complex of social class differences. These differences are highly associated with occupations, size of income, the manner in

[3] For some of these analyses, see Max Weber in Talcott Parsons (ed.), *The Theory of Social and Economic Organization*, (New York: Oxford, 1947); Kingsley Davis, "A Conceptual Analysis of Stratification," *American Sociological Review*, 7 (1942): 309-321; Talcott Parsons, "An Analytical Approach to the Theory of Social Stratification," *American Journal of Sociology*, 45 (1940): 841-862; Lucio Mendieta y Nunez, "The Social Classes," *American Sociological Review*, 11 (1946): 166-176; Charles H. Cooley, *Social Organization* (New York: Scribner's 1929); Herbert Goldhamer and Edward Shils, "Types of Power and Status," *American Journal of Sociology*, 45 (1939): 171-182; John F. Cuber and William F. Kenkel, *Social Stratification in United States* (New York: Appleton-Century-Crofts, 1954); Milton Gordon, *Social Class* (Durham: Duke University Press, 1958); Joseph Kahl, *The American Class Structure* (New York: Rinehart, 1957). Numerous other items may be found in Reinhard Bendix and Seymour Lipset, *Class, Status and Power: A Reader in Social Stratification* (New York: Free Press, 1953).

which income is received, level of education, and place of residence. These socio-economic variables are generally used as criteria for social class.

In addition to the social class criteria identified above, we must recognize that racial and ethnic classifications are also related to social class. Most Negroes and Mexican-Americans have generally been identified in the lower social class strata of our society. These minority groups also find it much more difficult to achieve higher social class status than do mobile members of the dominant group.

Although sociologists may have overemphasized the differences between classes in recent decades, it seems quite clear that class is associated with some differences in behavior. The nature of the family system and the concomitant socialization of the children may vary significantly from one class to another. Numerous analyses of public opinion and voting, as well as other types of behavior, have demonstrated significant differences between various social classes. Comparatively speaking, the American social class system is decidedly more open than stratification systems in many other societies. The possibility of movement from one stratum to another is a significant feature of the American stratification system. Social class identification in America is therefore to a considerable extent achieved by individuals and families and is not rigidly fixed by birth. The ideal of American culture involves a free movement and equality of opportunity for all people to move in the social class system. We sometimes verbalize the ideal that there are no differences of prestige or power in the society, but the evidence is quite clear that this is not the case. The expression of belief that Americans are all alike or about the same is the verbalization of an ideal that we readily recognize does not exist. The ideal of equality and particularly the equality of opportunity to move in the class system has tended to reduce the differences between people in various social categories. At the same time, there are significant forces tending to maintain the differences. The fact that a significant portion of the population is constantly striving to achieve higher status implies that the differences do exist and are recognized in the society. To some degree these differences are necessary if people are to be motivated to move in the class system. If people were actually all alike and equal in prestige and power, there would be no basis on which one could improve his position in the society.

The educational system has been intimately related to all aspects of the social class system.[4] Although occupation is highly correlated with social class in the United States, the educational level is closely intertwined with the process of social mobility. Prerequisite to attaining many higher prestige occupations in American society is the achievement of specific levels of education. In light of this, educational achievement is widely recognized as the primary means for achievement of higher social class status. Associated with this of course is the belief that education should provide a maximum degree of equality of opportunity to move into various positions in American society.

There is overpowering evidence that the American educational system has provided both an avenue for upward mobility and a degree of common cultural experience. Many people from lower socio-economic levels including those with minority group, racial, or ethnic identification have used the channels of educational achievement to enhance their social positions. At the same time there is much evidence that the common school experience which has been provided in many communities has tended to reduce the differences between children of various socio-economic statuses.[5] The schools may provide a common social-cultural experience within which the children from various strata may acquire an acquaintance across social class categories.

While the school system has provided the means for movement and the reduction of differences between social classes, it has also functioned as a means for maintaining differentiation and the allocation of children to various social

---

[4] See Wilbur Brookover and David Gottlieb, *A Sociology of Education* (American Book Company, 1964), Chapter 7 for an analysis of the relation of social class to education.

[5] *Ibid.*, p. 174 ff.

class strata. As we noted in previous discussions, the educational system has functioned to allocate personnel to the various social class categories. This has been achieved through a multitude of decisions related to the level and type of education which young people have been permitted or advised to take. Thus the system of testing, evaluating, selection, and admission to various schools and curricula are all a part of the process by which the educational system differentiates among those who were channeled into various positions and social strata of the society.[6] Children from lower socio-economic categories have frequently been identified as less able to learn the kinds of behavior taught in school. This presumption of limited and inferior learning ability frequently leads to the assignment of lower class children to differentiated curricula and lower tracks that do not culminate in higher educational opportunities. They make up a large proportion of the non-college bound students.

Sub-Cultural Variation vs.
Cultural Deprivation

We have identified thus far a series of sub-society or sub-cultural categories in American society and noted the relationship of education to the various sub-cultural variations. The various ethnic, regional, and socio-economic categories of American children may cause some to be disadvantaged in learning the types of behavior that are emphasized in American schools. These disadvantages in the educational milieu have frequently been identified as cultural deprivation. One implication of the latter concept is that these children have been deprived of a culture. As we have noted, this of course is not the case but they have had the kind of pre-school and other childhood experiences that are not to their advantage in the school setting. The culturally or educationally disadvantaged are therefore simply composed of the children from

[6] See Hugh Kariger, "The Relationship of Lane Grouping to the Socioeconomic Status of Parents," PhD Thesis, Michigan State University, 1962. Also W. B. Brookover, Don Leu, and Hugh Kariger, "Discrimination in Tracking." *Phi Delta Kappan*, Spring 1969.

sub-societies in which the kinds of behavior most appropriate for school learning have not been learned. Such disadvantages are found among several sub-cultural categories. In all of these, the particular sub-societies have a highly developed and complex sub-culture which is functional for the situation in which the children live. They are, however, generally disadvantaged in the typical American school. The language, vocabulary, and other kinds of behavior patterns they acquire in their subcultures do not facilitate the school learning objectives.

Lower class sub-societies, of course, contribute the largest share of educationally disadvantaged children. It would be a serious mistake, however, to automatically assume that all lower class children are educationally disadvantaged. Many children from poor families are high achievers. The danger is that stereotypes of lower class sub-cultures as educationally disadvantaged or culturally deprived may inadvertently contribute to the educational handicaps of lower class children. This is especially true when the stereotypes are negative. The problem is to recognize the contributions of sub-cultures to school performance without overdrawing our generalizations. In a later section of this chapter we will attempt to enumerate characteristics of the lower class which tend to handicap children.

SUB-CULTURAL DIVERSITY AND SCHOOL LEARNING

We have examined briefly the history of American educational policy with regard to cultural differences and identified some of the significant sub-societies within the larger society. The implications of these sub-society differences for school learning depend on several social forces both within and external to the sub-societies. The systematic study of these forces has been very limited, but some of the factors which affect learning in school can be identified. Among these are (1) the goals or desires of both the dominant segment of the society and the particular sub-society involved, (2) the power of the sub-society in relation to the power of the controlling segment of the society, (3) the degree of diversity between the sub-society and the dominant elements of the society, and (4) the particular assets or deficits which the children bring to the schools. We shall examine each of these factors briefly.

Dominant and Subordinate Group Agreement

The performance and behavior of the children of the sub-society are affected to some degree by the goals which the particular sub-society has with regard to the education of its youth. As we have noted earlier, the organization of the schools and the performance of the sub-groups are also affected by the policy or goals which the dominant society holds for the particular sub-group. In this regard we have noted that the American policy has varied from time to time and with regard to different sub-cultural segments of the larger society. If both the sub-society and the dominant policy-making segment of the society desire to maintain a separate culture, it is likely to be reflected in the school organization. If both the sub-society and the dominant controlling interests wish the sub-group to become acculturated and integrated into the total society, the organization of schools is also likely to facilitate this process and it will occur rapidly. The children of the sub-group will in this case acquire the dominant cultural patterns within a generation or so.

Dominant and Subordinate Group Conflict

When the sub-society's goals are different from those of the controlling segment of the larger society, the learning of the children and the organization of the schools will no doubt depend on other forces. If the sub-society wishes to lose its identity and become a part of the larger society, the extent to which its children will acquire the behavior of the dominant groups depends on the power of the dominant segment to maintain separate schools for this minority and deny them the opportunity to acquire its culture. The power to do this will be affected by the degree of diversity or the extent to which the sub-cultural population can be identified and set apart in different schools or segments of the school. If the minority sub-group cannot be readily identified, a significant proportion of the children may acquire the dominant culture in spite of the efforts to prevent this. If, on the other hand, the diverse sub-society members can be readily identified by race or other characteristics, the dominant group may be able to maintain the denial of access to their culture for extended periods.

If the minority sub-society wishes to maintain its diversity while the dominant group wishes to integrate it, the extent to which the children will acquire the dominant culture depends on the cohesiveness of the minority group and its ability to isolate its children from the influences of the controlling interests of the society. Religious sects such as the Amish have been able to do this to a considerable extent over a long period of time.

In our discussion of the goals of both the dominant and the divergent groups, we have recognized the importance of the relative power of the groups. In general, the operation of the power system depends on the agreement or disagreement of the dominant and divergent sub-society with regard to goals or purposes. The American Indian sub-cultures in the United States have been relatively powerless compared to the centralized power of the Federal Government. Until recently, black Americans have had little power to determine the educational program for their youth. As we shall note in Chapter 6, the mobilization of power both within the Negro society and segments of the white stratum has greatly affected this balance of power. The particular outcome of the educational program will vary not only with the relative power but also with the degree to which the sub-society's goals concur with those of the dominant group. In general, Negroes in American society have desired equality with whites and have wished to become integrated into the total American society, but some forces are now operating to teach and maintain a separate Afro-American culture.

In addition to the degree of diversity, the particular patterns of culturally defined behavior which children acquire may affect the degree to which they function adequately in school. Jewish and Japanese-American children have generally not been handicapped in the acquisition of the behavior taught in American schools. In fact it appears that the achievement-motivation characteristic of these sub-cultures has enhanced the performance of Jewish and Japanese-American children in the academic arena. Although some sub-cultures seem to have a significant advantage in the performance of those types of behavior emphasized in school, other sub-cultural differences are a disadvantage in the acquisition of the behavior characteristic of the school program.

Educational Disadvantages of Poverty

The disadvantage of children coming from the lower socio-economic categories derives in part at least from the fact that such children have had little or no experience with books or written language; in contrast with members of sub-societies who have high levels of education, the lower socio-economic groups do not provide models of reading behavior and the environment is not characterized by emphasis on books, magazines, and related materials involved in the school. Such children do not acquire, prior to entering school, a high value on reading and related behaviors nor do they have skill in handling and manipulating the objects connected with such behavior.

Another difference among sub-societies which is closely related to the commonly developed processes of school learning is the difference in language; children coming from sub-societies where the adults have high levels of education learn the language that is commonly used in school. The vocabulary and sentence structure found among teachers and in the school reading material is familiar. In contrast, children from other sub-societies may have had little or no interaction with people who use the formal language of the school. Rather, these children acquire the language of the sub-society of which they are a part. The vocabulary and range of modifying terms and style of language may be decidedly different. In his analysis, Bernstein identifies the language of the lower class British as the "public" or "restricted" language. He maintains that the children from families with higher levels of education will learn both the "formal or elaborated" language of the educational system and the public language of the streets. Bernstein characterized the public language as follows:

1. Short, grammatically simple, often unfinished sentences with a poor syntactical form stressing the active voice.
2. Simple and repetitive use of conjunctions (so, then, because).
3. Little use of subordinate clauses to break down the initial categories of the dominant subject.
4. Inability to hold a formal subject through a speech sequence; thus facilitating a dislocated informational content.
5. Rigid and limited use of adjectives and adverbs.
6. Infrequent use of impersonal pronoun as subjects of conditional clauses or sentences e.g. "one."
7. Frequent use of statements where the reason and conclusion are confounded to produce a categoric utterance.
8. A large number of statements or phrases which signal a requirement for the previous speech sequence to be reinforced: "Wouldn't it? You see? You know?" etc. This process is termed "sympathetic circularity."
9. Individual selection from a group of idiomatic phrases or sequences will frequently occur.
10. The individual qualification is implicit in the sentence organization; it is a language of implicit meaning.

On the other hand, the *elaborated* language is characterized by:

1. Accurate grammatical order and syntax regulate what is said.
2. Logical modifications and stress are mediated through a grammatically complex sentence construction, especially through the use of a range of conjunctions and subordinate clauses.

3. Frequent use of prepositions which indicate logical relationship as well as prepositions which indicate temporal and spatial contiguity.

4. Frequent use of the impersonal pronoun "it," one.

5. A descriminative selection from a range of adjectives and adverbs.

6. Individual qualification is verbally mediated through the structure and relationships within and between sentences.

7. Expressive symbolism discriminates between meanings within speech sequences rather than reinforcing specific dominant words or phrases, and/or accompanying the sequence in a generalized diffuse, manner.

8. A language use which points to the possibilities inherent in a complex conceptual hierarchy for the organizing of experience.[7]

To the extent that the more common cultural norms of behavior in various sub-societies are in harmony with those of the educational system, the child from these groups may be advantaged in acquiring the patterns of behavior taught in school. Also, to the extent that the common norms of behavior in sub-societies are divergent or different from those that are expected in the school, the children may be disadvantaged in school learning. The language acquired is probably more crucial than any other aspects of behavior.

In addition to the disadvantages of children from sub-societies whose norms and appropriate behavior do not converge closely with those of the school, educators in America have sometimes added the belief that such children should not be expected to learn the same types of behavior in school that others do. This is associated with our emphasis on individual differences and individual needs. Since a child from a Negro or poor lower-class white family does not readily learn to read the formal language and other types of behavior, we frequently conclude that it is inappropriate to ask him to learn

[7] Reprinted from Basil Bernstein, "Social Class and Linguistic Development: A Theory of Social Learning;" in A. H. Halsey, Jean Floud and C. Arnold Anderson, Education, Economy and Society, pp. 297-298 and 311, by permission of the Publisher (Copyright 1961. Free Press of Glencoe).

such behavior. Educators thus hold different expectations and norms of school learning for children from disadvantaged sub-cultures.[8] Since we do not think it is appropriate for all the children to learn the same behavior, we devise different curricula and other educational experiences for the children who are not expected to learn the academic types of behavior. Associated with this variation in the school's definition of appropriate learning for various sub-cultural groups is a differential perception of learning ability. When American-Indian, Negro, rural, or children from lower socio-economic categories do not readily learn the kinds of behavior that children from the other sub-societies learn readily, the teacher is likely to identify such children as unable to learn these kinds of behavior. Since a child is defined as having limited ability, the teacher is therefore justified in not asking him to learn what children from other sub-cultures learn.

Teachers and educators generally are highly committed to the value of education for all children and believe it is desirable to provide opportunity for all children through the educational process. As we have indicated, however, the system tends to differentiate between the education provided for children from differing sub-societies. The differences in the common cultural learnings of a child before he enters school affect the readiness with which the child adapts to the school learning situation, and these differences in turn become the basis for differential definitions of appropriate learning and differential perceptions of learning ability.

SUGGESTED READINGS

BERNSTEIN, BASIL, "Social Class and Linguistic Development: A Theory of Social Learning" in A. H. Halsey, Jean Floud, and C. Arnold Anderson, *Education, Economy and Society*, N.Y.: Free Press of Glencoe, 1961, pp. 288-314.

[8] *See* Robert Rosenthal and Lenore Jacobson, *Pygmalion in the Classroom*, New York, Holt, Rinehart and Winston, 1968, for an analysis of the effect of teachers' expectations on learning.

CLARK, BURTON R., *Educating the Expert Society*. San Francisco: Chandler Publishing Company, 1962. A sociological analysis of the social aspects of educational structures, their social causes and their consequences.

COUNTS, GEORGE S., *Education and American Civilization*, New York: Bureau of Publications, Teachers College, Columbia University, 1952, pp. XIV-491.

GORDON, EDMUND and DOXEY A. WILKERSON, *Compensatory Education for the Disadvantaged*. New York: College Entrance Examination Board, 1966. A summary and analysis of subcultural and school environments and a critical evaluation of compensatory education programs for disadvantaged groups.

HANNA, PAUL R. (ed.), *Education: An Instrument of National Goals*. New York: McGraw-Hill Book Co., 1962.

CHAPTER

4

Group Norms
and
Expectations

WE DO NOT LEARN directly from such abstract categories as *society* or *culture*. Rather, each of us learns his culture from particular groups and persons. If each of us has a unique set of experiences with others, each of us is bound to be unique in outlook and behavior. Conversely, if each of us shares experiences with others, each is likely to conform in outlook and behavior. Hence, to understand the unique and common characteristics of students involves a knowledge of the groups and persons with whom students interact. In this chapter, we shall turn our attention to those persons and groups most likely to affect the behavior of children and adolescents of school age.

TYPES OF GROUPS

▶ *Ascribed vs. Voluntary Groups.* One way of viewing or classifying groups is by distinguishing between ascribed and voluntary group membership. Membership in ascribed groups is not by choice of the members. An ascribed group is best illustrated by age and sex groups. All females in a given society are ascribed members of a broad category of persons simply because they are female. Likewise, identification as a male ascribes a person to another category or group.[1]

Although not as sharply defined, age categories are also the basis for ascribed group identification. Children and adolescents are not members or participants in adult groups. The exact time at which we cease to be a child and become an adolescent or cease to be an adolescent and become an adult is not as precisely identified in American society as it is in some others. The behavior ascribed to these age categories is significantly different. Some have identified the age categories as sub-societies or sub-cultures, but it is clear that these social categories are somewhat different from the sub-societies which were discussed in Chapter 3.

In contrast to groups based on ascribed biological and psychological statuses, there are a larger number of social groups which are based on the choices and achievements of the persons involved. Some voluntary groups are formally identified and may be named. Others are informal and are based solely on the individual's patterns of interaction and his feelings about relationships to other people.

▶ *Reference Groups.* Another related but distinctly different basis for classifying groups is the fact that individuals may take the standard of a particular group to evaluate or judge themselves. An individual, for example, may adopt a group's criterion as to what is handsome in assessing his own handsomeness. The group whose standard the individual adopts is the individual's reference group.[2] It is important to note that one can be a member of a group which is not his reference

---

[1] *See* Richard Dewey and W. J. Humber, *An Introduction to Social Psychology* (New York: The Macmillan Company, 1966, pp. 104-121 for an analysis of groups and significant others.

[2] G. H. Mead used the concept "generalized other" to refer to the abstract group to which the individual referred for evaluation. This is similar in meaning to the concept reference group. See *Mind, Self and Society* (Chicago: University of Chicago Press, 1934).

group. A group may be both a membership group and a reference group to a particular person, but need not be both. The latter is illustrated by a high-school student who is a member of one clique in his school but uses the standards of another clique to judge himself. The distinction is made to emphasize the fact that observable associations of a person are not necessarily the most relevant ones affecting his behavior.

▶ *Significant Others.* The concept "reference group" is closely related, although not synonymous, with the concept "significant other." Significant other is used in the singular to identify real or imaginary persons who influence the individual's beliefs about himself and his world. In this sense the two concepts have similar meanings, although reference group has a group connotation and significant other more commonly has an individual connotation.

It is important to recognize that the relevant reference group or significant other may vary from one situation to another. In one situation, for example, students' occupational aspirations, the parents may be the ones whose perceived expectations and evaluations are of most concern to the child. In another area of behavior, for example students' dating patterns, the child's schoolmates or peer group may be the most significant. In some areas of behavior, the expectations of two or more reference groups or significant others may be perceived as equally valid by the child. In such instances, one set of expectations may reinforce the other, but in some situations the expectations may be perceived as incompatible. In the latter, the person often attempts to resolve the perceived conflict in some manner.[3] Situations in which two or more significant others are perceived to hold incompatible expectations are generally identified as one form of role conflict. Such situations will be discussed in greater detail later.

▶ *Adolescent Groups.* There is not always a clear distinction between sub-societies and the social aggregates or groups

[3] *See* Wilbur Brookover and David Gottlieb, *A Sociology of Education,* Chapter 12 for discussion of role conflict.

which make up the sub-societies. The members of one sub-society or stratum frequently perceive other sub-societies as if there were no differentiated groups within that sub-society. Some white Americans, for example, frequently classify all American Indians as essentially alike. In fact, however, there are many sub-societies or sub-cultural groups within the broader American-Indian population. The Amish in the United States are also frequently perceived as a relatively small homogeneous sub-society. This is correct in the sense that there are common cultural patterns of behavior among the various Amish communities. It must be recognized, however, that in the total Amish sub-society there are many groups or communities that can be easily differeniated in terms of the norms of behavior and the type of religious beliefs which are maintained.[4] An analysis of the behavior and patterns of socialization within the Amish communities would, therefore, necessitate a recognition of the differences among the numerous Amish groups. Although the outsiders may not recognize these differences, the members of the various groups readily distinguish members of one group from those of another by particular behavior patterns and symbols. The symbols frequently involve variations in clothing.

The distinction between a sub-society and a group is relevant to our discussion at this point, because we have chosen to analyze the school "society" and its attendant cultural patterns as one of several possible student groups. This is not in accord with several other scholars who have identified adolescents as making up a sub-society with divergent cultural patterns.[5] Others have further subdivided the high-school and college societies into what might be termed "sub-sub-cultures." Such classifications are based on the fact that it is possible to identify differences in values and behavior between the adolescent and adult segments of American culture. Al-

---

[4] See John Hostetler, *Amish Society* (Baltimore: John Hopkins Press, 1963) for an excellent analysis of the Amish.

[5] Among these are James Coleman, *The Adolescent Society* (New York: The Free Press of Glencoe, 1961); Coleman, *The Adolescent and the School.* (New York: Basic Books, 1965).

though we concur in the differentiation of peer and adult influences, we believe the differences have been somewhat exaggerated. Perhaps it is inappropriate to generally label adolescent groups as representing a sub-culture. Sub-culture has generally included a means of socializing persons into and maintaining membership in the sub-culture. The adolescent stage is a transitory stage involving socialization to wider community practices and beliefs.

Although we do not wish to minimize its importance, we would emphasize that the adolescent age group is not a complete sub-society in the sense that the Amish are a sub-society. Our first consideration will be an examination of sources of student influence.

THE IDENTIFICATION OF STUDENTS' SIGNIFICANT OTHERS

Two major questions are relevant: (1) Who are the significant others and reference groups of students? and (2) what are the students' perceptions of these significant others and reference groups? That is, what do the students think their reference groups expect of them as students? There is increasing literature designed to answer these questions for the high-school and college age groups in America, but there is very little sound evidence on which to answer such questions concerning younger elementary age students. This may result from the assumption that parents are by and large the most significant others for the elementary age group and that teachers largely function as parent surrogates in the elementary classrooms. These may be accurate assumptions, but we are not in a position to verify them with very much sound research evidence.

The research on the secondary school, and to a lesser extent on the college level, has assumed that students' age-grade peers provide the primary and dominant point of reference for these categories of students. Coleman, for example, assumes that age-grade peers are the dominating source of influence on adolescents.

This setting-apart of our children in school—which take on ever more functions, ever more "extra curricular activities"—for an ever longer period of training has a singular impact on the child of high-school age. He is "cut off" from the rest of society, forced inward toward his own age group, made to carry out his whole social life with others his own age. With his fellows, he comes to constitute a small society, one that has most of its important interactions *within* itself, and maintains only a few threads of connection with the outside adult society. In our modern world of mass communication and rapid diffusion of ideas and knowledge, it is hard to realize that separate sub-cultures can exist right under the very noses of adults—sub-cultures with languages all their own, with special symbols, and, most importantly, with value systems that may differ from adults.[6]

Coleman here implies that the norms and expectations of the adolescents not only are different in some respects from the adults', but also are controlling in regard to the academic behavior of adolescents. Although the peer group provides a significant portion of social interaction, we should not overlook the fact that students also interact extensively with other segments of society through both the mass communication and personal face-to-face contacts. In fact, children and adolescents in American schools probably continue greater contact with adults outside the school, and particularly family members, than do students in some other societies where boarding schools are more common.

In an earlier period when America was largely a rural society and the means of transportation and communication were limited, children and youth of school age interacted with a relatively narrow circle of associates. There was a continuous interaction with parents and siblings, and frequently with other family members, as well as with a small circle of neighbors. In general, the circle of others with whom the student interacted held similar expectations for their behavior. This was also true of the teachers who usually came from the same community or

[6] Reprinted from James S. Coleman, *The Adolescent Society*, p. 3, by permission of the Publishers (Copyright 1962, The Free Press of Glencoe).

a similar one nearby. In this context, the child in school had interaction with people who held a relatively homogeneous set of expectations and the circle of interaction was small. In contemporary industrialized America with its high degree of specialization, the child has less continuous interaction with parents. The members of the family, particularly the father, work away from home and the child has contact with a much wider circles of associates. Because of this, the child may have interaction with people who come from different groups and sub-societies which hold varying expectations for children and youth. In contemporary American society, therefore, it is not easy to determine which of the several groups and individuals the student interacts with is the more relevant. At times, the age-grade peers may be the most relevant referent. Under other circumstances, teachers, parents, other adults, or even distant individuals may be the student's guiding influence.

With little foundation on which to base a conclusion, some writers dealing with the adolescent period have assumed that the adolescent peer group is the dominant and perhaps the only significant group affecting the behavior of adolescent boys and girls regardless of the behavior in question.[7] In societies with an extensive range of interaction such as we have in the United States, the significant group or persons may vary greatly from one situation to another. For example, the adolescent may employ peer group values in his evaluation of himself as a dancer. This same student may also use the standards of his parents or other adults to appraise his performance in algebra or history.

▶ *Persons Perceived to be Important and Concerned.* The authors and their colleagues have sought to identify the significant others for academic behavior for a population of students in their junior and senior high schools in a midwestern city of over 100,000 population. Partial information on this problem was obtained by asking the students to respond to

[7] *See* James S. Coleman, *Adolescent and the Schools* (New York: Basic Books, 1965), particularly chapter 2.

the following questions each year while in grades eight through twelve.

"There are many people who are important in our lives. In the space below, list the NAMES of the people who you feel are important in YOUR life. Please indicate who each person is."

and:

"There are many people who are concerned about how well young people do in school. In the space below, list the NAMES of the people you feel are concerned about how well you do in school. Please indicate who each person is."

These questions were intended to elicit identification of persons who were perceived as generally important to the respondent and also those who were particularly oriented to the area of academic behavior in school. The answers of 561 students who responded to these questions each year, beginning in the eighth grade, are presented in Tables 1 and 2.[8]

Almost the entire class named parents as being important in their lives and concerned about how well they performed in school throughout their junior and senior high-school years. Although one might question the formulation of the questions used and the assumption that students will give valid answers rather than the expected answers, there is little indication that the age-grade friends of the respondents are the dominant influence. The proportion who named one or more age-grade friends varies somewhat from one year to another but at no time does it approximate the proportion who named parents in response to either question. This casts some doubt on the assumption that adolescents are the most important influence on students' behavior.

Other investigations of student indications of persons whose judgment they value with regard to clothing, musical interests, and other adolescent-oriented activities indicate that

8 W. B. Brookover, Edsel Erickson, and Lee Joiner, *Concept of Ability and School Achievement III.* Report of Cooperative Research Project 2831, Bureau of Publication Services (East Lansing: Michigan State University, 1967), pp. 107-109.

age-grade friends are somewhat more likely to be named by high-school students when concerned about these types of behavior. However, the vast majority of students also named parents as significant others in reference to these areas of behavior.

Also, as indicated in Tables 1 and 2, a large proportion of students identify others in addition to their parents and friends as being generally important in their lives. These findings reflect the considerable range of student interaction with people whom they perceive as important and concerned about their academic performance. Although these findings do not measure directly the student's reference groups, it seems reasonable to conclude from them that for many secondary-school students the family, neighbors, and other adult groups may all contribute to the criterion by which the students determine what is appropriate to learn as well as to assess their competencies to learn. Certainly there is no reason to conclude that only one person or one reference group is solely responsible for a student's perceptions of self as a student.

The student in school not only interacts with a wide range of people in contemporary American society, but also functions in numerous roles or statuses in the process of inter-action. The roles include a son or a daughter, a brother or a sister, a student in a particular grade or school, a child in the neighborhood, a playmate, a boy friend or a girl friend. In these roles, the student interacts with age-grade associates and neighbors as well as with parents and other family members. The average American child or adolescent is also a member of various informal cliques or crowds within which he performs particular roles. In addition to the family and student roles, the child may function in various school-related or non-school clubs such as the 4H club, the Boy or Girl Scouts, or numerous recreational activities. In each of these groups, the child or adolescent functions in relation to the expectations which the relevant others hold for him in the particular role. On numerous occasions more than one group may hold varying expecta-tions for him. Although the expectations of the parents may take precedence in the child's role as a son or daughter, it is

TABLE 1

Percentage of the Same Students at Each Grade Level Who Name at Least One Person
in Each of the Following Categories of Significant Others as Being *Important in Their Lives*

Males = 255 and Females = 306

Categories of Others "General Significant Others"	Sex	Grade 8 %	Grade 9 %	Grade 10 %	Grade 11 %	Grade 12 %
Parent (s)	Males	97	96	96	95	93
	Females	99	98	96	98	98
Age Level Relatives:	Males	62	60	46	52	57
	Females	76	75	70	78	75
Adult Relatives:	Males	38	40	27	35	31
	Females	55	57	47	53	52
Friends, Same Sex:	Males	44	48	26	33	27
	Females	54	68	46	62	53
Friends, Opposite Sex:	Males	15	18	14	22	26
	Females	30	32	33	57	25
Local Adults:	Males	19	20	15	20	24
	Females	27	32	23	23	16
Teachers in General:	Males	38	37	24	20	18
	Females	34	34	12	16	16
Other Academic Persons: (Counselors, coaches, principals)	Males	9	9	6	13	15
	Females	12	6	3	7	7
Unclassified: (e.g. God, famous people, dogs, me, etc.)	Males	28	22	18	25	16
	Females	12	17	13	15	12

TABLE 2

Percentage of the Same Students at Each Grade Level Who Name at Least One Person in Each of the Following Categories of Significant Others as Being Concerned About How Well They do in School

Males = 255 and Females = 306

Categories of Others "Academic Significant Others"	Sex	Grade 8 %	Grade 9 %	Grade 10 %	Grade 11 %	Grade 12 %
Parent (s)	Males	96	97	96	95	96
	Females	99	99	98	98	97
Age Level Relatives:	Males	19	30	20	26	29
	Females	24	38	29	42	45
Adult Relatives:	Males	30	37	31	29	27
	Females	45	55	41	52	31
Friends, Same Sex:	Males	5	8	6	10	11
	Females	11	21	17	30	39
Friends, Opposite Sex:	Males	4	7	5	13	21
	Females	4	9	16	31	16
Local Adults:	Males	4	5	5	7	10
	Females	6	11	7	14	19
Teachers in General:	Males	60	53	44	34	26
	Females	63	50	35	35	29
Other Academic Persons: (Counselors, coaches, principals)	Males	29	27	33	33	18
	Females	37	33	33	33	32
Unclassified: (e.g. God, famous people, dogs, me, etc.)	Males	35	23	24	30	25
	Females	37	30	32	22	25

clear that the expectations held by neighbors and other members of the family are not irrelevant for a child's behavior in this role. In a similar fashion, several people hold expectations for the individual as a student in school. Parents, teachers, peers, other members of the family, neighbors, and many others have expectations for the child's behavior both in elementary and secondary school classroom and extra-classroom activities. The same may be said of almost any role in which a person functions.

The multiple role expectations may require the student to behave in terms of two or more roles at the same time. Thus, the same significant other or reference group may expect the child to be both a good student and an obedient son or daughter at the time and under the same kinds of circumstances. At another stage, the parents may expect a son to function as a good student and a good athlete at the same time.

The multiplicity of roles and of persons and groups which hold expectations for the student has led to a considerable discussion of the possible similarities and conflicts in these expectations and the relative importance of each of them. One gets the impression from the literature on adolescence that the expectations of adults and the adolescent peers vary greatly and are frequently in conflict.

In other words, we believe the assumed conflict in parental and friendship expectations has been extrapolated far beyond sound data. The fact that adolescent norms and behavior can be differentiated to some extent from those of adults has led to presumption that adult expectations are in conflict with the expectations of the adolescent peer group. The adolescent peer group's emphasis on athletics, fun, good personality, and a variety of other behavior has led to the conclusion that students do not anticipate or expect their peers to perform well in school while teachers and parents hold such expectations for them. Evidence presented in Chapter 5 does not support the conflict thesis.

It is an over simplification to speak of either parents, friends, or teachers as having more or less general influence on students' behavior. As stated in the discussion of reference

groups, friends may well have more influence on students'
dating patterns while parents may be the most significant
others affecting how their children evaluate their career
chances. The general influence of others on career choices
may vary by age of children, ability to communicate, extent
of surveillance, and many other factors. As will be noted in the
next chapter, the parents of deaf institutionalized high-school
children seem to have less influence on their children's self-
concept of academic ability than do parents of non-impaired
children in public schools.

Perceived Evaluations and Expectations
Held by Significant Others

In order to assess the impact of others' expectations and
perceived evaluations on a person's behavior, we should know
what these others desire of the student and how they evaluate
his ability. Even more important, we should know the student's
perceptions of expectations and evaluations of others. If significant others act as if the student is capable of performing in
accord with their preferences for him, the student is likely to
carry out their desires. While there is evidence that students'
perception of others' expectations and evaluations for self are
highly correlated with the actual expectations and evaluations
of these others, there is, however, some communication failure
and it should be noted that individuals behave in terms of
what they perceive of others and not in terms of the actual
expectations and assessments that others hold.

In a recent study of public school students, in grades seven,
eight, nine, and ten, it was concluded that the parental evaluations of students' academic ability were more highly related
to students' self-conceptions of academic ability than were
friends' evaluations of students.[9] In grade eleven, the parents
and friends seemed to have an equal impact on students' self-
concept of ability. In grade twelve, the evaluations of friends

[9] Brookover, W. B., Edsel Erickson, and Lee Joiner, 1967, *op. cit.*
pp. 107-109.

in contrast to parents were slightly more related to students' self-concept of ability. From grades seven through twelve, the impact of parental evaluations on self-concept of ability was greater than that of teacher evaluations. We must be careful, however, in the way in which we interpret these findings. First, no conclusion is warranted that one or the other group has no influence or cannot increase its influence. The evaluations of all three groups, parents, friends and teachers, accounted for some of the variation in students' self-concept independent of one another. In addition, parents, friends, and teachers often shared the same evaluations of students so that the importance of one group or another cannot be readily discerned.

Conditions Affecting the
Influence of Others

A second problem in understanding the relative influence of others' expectations and evaluations on students, concerns an adequate assessment of the conditions which modify the impact of these evaluations and expectations. It is quite possible, for instance, that a parent may communicate to his son that he ought to get B's in school but, more important, he ought to make the first string of the varsity football team.

Another parent may communicate to his son that he ought to get B's in school and that getting B's is more important than anything else he might do in school. In other words, the relative importance that others attach to their expectations of students can influence the impact of those expectations.

Another factor, which may affect the influence of expectations, is the extent to which the individual perceives that others will be aware of whether or not he carries out their expectations. Two sets of parents can both desire B's on the part of their children. They can place equal importance on getting B grades in school, but one set of parents may not have its child's school behavior under close surveillance while the other parents may be much aware of what and how well their child is doing in school. The parents who are more aware of how their child is doing in school are in a position to reinforce through approval or sanction the desired or undesirable academic behavior. Certainly, if the student does not think others are or will be aware of whether or not he carries out their expectations of him, there is nothing compelling about these expectations.

The comparison of the expectations of parents and friends concerning a particular activity is not likely to provide valid evidence of the influence of these groups unless the degree of importance and surveillance attached to the expectations by each are also examined. Parents may tend to prefer certain achievement levels on the part of students which may or may not differ from friends' preferences for students. If they do differ, it is rather "far-fetched" to infer that there is any meaningful conflict on the part of the student, or that one group's expectations are more relevant than another group's, unless one knows that there are conditions of importance and surveillance attached to these expectations. Importance and surveillance are conditions which tend to obligate the individual to carry out the expectations of others. If others do not place much importance on their desires for the student or they are perceived to be unaware of whether or not these desires are met, there is no social obligation to carry out their desires.[10]

Without questioning the fact that peers may exert considerable influence in many areas, the assertion that parents are not an important influence on the academic achievement of students is unfounded. The relationships of students to friends are not as likely to involve obligations for achievement beyond staying in school as are their relation to parents. That is, friends are simply not likely to make a particular level of academic achievement a condition for continued friendship. Parents on the other hand are likely to emphasize the importance of achievement at some level even though it may be only the C expected by Willy Loman in *Death of a Salesman*.

[10] *Ibid.*, Chapter IX, pp. 191-204; and Edsel Erickson, *A Study of the Normative Influence on Parents and Friends on Academic Achievement* (doctoral dissertation, East Lansing: Michigan State University, 1965).

The absence of extensive conflict in the expectations held by parents and high-school friends is further indicated by a study of tenth graders in a midwestern city. Only eight out of 942 students in this group reported that parents held high academic achievement expectations while friends held low achievement expectations or vice versa under conditions in which they felt obligated to fulfill the expectations of both parties. More than one-fourth of these students felt that their parents considered the expected level of achievement important and kept a close surveillance over them. Less than 10 per cent felt that their friends placed such conditions of obligation on their achievement expectations. The academic expectations which these students perceived that their parents and friends held for them were similar for all but eight students. Less than one per cent of these high-school students were faced with academic role conflict between parents and friends in which they felt obligated to perform in accord with different expectations.

We have noted that there is a wide range of people who may be significant points of reference with whom the school-aged child and adolescent may interact. The failure of many students to achieve at a high level in school has led various scholars and teachers to suggest that some group or significant others are responsible for the low achievement. Teachers frequently indicate that lower-class parents have low expectations and aspirations for their children while parents from higher status levels may expect too much from their children. This suggests vast differences in the school achievement expected of school-age children. Although our evidence is meager, we believe that the presumed conflicts and differences have been greatly exaggerated. Most parents at all socioeconomic levels, we believe, desire that their children do well in school. Lower class parents, however, may not see high academic attainments as a possibility for their children and, therefore, not sanction and reward academic behaviors as much as middle and upper class parents. Similarly, we do not believe that most high-school adolescents desire their peers to fail or to do poorly in school. And should the case be that the academic achievements of students are less relevant to friends than parents, this is hardly a basis for asserting parent-friend conflict.

Although we question the assumed conflict between parents and school expectations, there is little question that the range of associations and the norms and expectations of the school society provide a significant referent for the students in school. It is, therefore, essential that we examine the nature of this social organization and the norms and expectations which characterize the school.

THE SCHOOL SOCIAL SYSTEM

► *The School as a Closed System.* The school social system is similar in many respects to "closed" social systems that are sometimes characterized as total institutions. Such institutions are separated from the larger society to a significant degree and carry out their functions with limited interaction with outside organizations. In varying degrees, such total institutions are illustrated by hospitals, military units, factories or other business units, and prisons as well as the schools. In each of these, there are two identifiable sub-systems. The nature of these two sub-units varies somewhat from one to another but they are characterized by a certain degree of difference in the amount of control or dominance which they have. The most extreme of these, of course, is the prison situation where the warden and his staff exerts almost absolute control and sets certain rules and regulations to govern the behavior of the prisoners. To a much lesser degree the same kind of distinction can be made between employer and employees in a factory. The hospital and the school are somewhat different, but the two segments of the system can be clearly identified. The doctors, nurses, and other staff members in a hospital are distinguished from and have different functions than the patients. The teachers, administrators, and other adult staff members of the school are clearly distinguishable from the students. In all of these, one group has the assigned tasks of directing and supervising the behavior of the other segment. The teachers are clearly identified as the directors, supervisors, or in a sense may be designated as the controllers of the controlled. In this instance, the teachers and other adults are the professional and sub-professional personnel to whom society has assigned certain tasks.[11] The teachers, like military officers, are the persons whom society holds responsible for the achievement of certain goals by the student participants in the institution.

▶ *The Teacher-Student Relationship.* The dual composition of the school as a total institution sets up a social system in which a contest is likely to develop. Similar to the prison or hospital situation, the students develop their own informal social groups, if not a formal organization, with student statuses, roles, and norms of behavior. The students' definition of appropriate behavior may be different from the norms and expectations held by the teachers who are assigned as the controllers of the social institution.

The institutionalized relationship between the teachers and the pupils in the school often produces a contest. One of the best analyses and descriptions of this situation was made by Willard Waller a number of years ago.

> The teacher-pupil relationship is a form of institutionalized dominance and subordination. Teacher and pupil confront each other in the school with an original conflict of desires, and however much that conflict may be reduced in amount, or however much it may be hidden, it still remains. The teacher represents the adult group, ever the enemy of the spontaneous life of groups of children. The teacher represents the formal curriculum, and his interest is in imposing that curriculum upon the children in the form of tasks; pupils are much more interested in life in their own world than in the desiccated bits of adult life which teachers have to offer. The teacher represents the established social order in the school, and his interest is in maintaining that order,

[11] *See* Irving Goffman, *Asylums* (Aldine Publishing Company, Chicago: 1967).

whereas pupils have only a negative interest in the feudal superstructure. Teacher and pupil confront each other with attitudes from which the underlying hostility can never be altogether removed. Pupils are the material in which teachers are supposed to produce results. Pupils are human beings striving to realize themselves in their own spontaneous manner, striving to produce their own results in their own way. Each of these hostile parties stands in the way of the other; in so far as the aims of either are realized, it is at the sacrifice of the aims of the other.

Authority is on the side of the teacher. The teacher nearly always wins. In fact, he must win or he cannot remain a teacher. Children after all, are usually docile, and they certainly are defenseless against the machinery with which the adult world is able to enforce its decisions; the result of the battle is foreordained. Conflict between teachers and students therefore passes to the second level. All the externals of conflict and of authority having been settled, the matter chiefly at issue is the meaning of those externals. Whatever the rules that the teacher lays down, the tendency of the pupils is to empty them of meaning. By mechanization of conformity, by "laughing off" the teacher or hating him out of all existence as a person, by taking refuge in self-initiated activities that are always just beyond the teacher's reach, students attempt to neutralize teacher control. The teacher, however, is striving to read meaning into the rules and regulations, to make standards really standards, to force students really to conform. This is a battle which is not unequal. The power of the teacher to pass rules is not limited, but his power to enforce rules is, and so is his power to control attitudes toward rules.[12]

Although contemporary teachers may feel that Waller's description of the contest and potential conflict is overdrawn, there is much evidence that the general structure of the school is reflected in this pattern of dominance and subordination. To understand the norms of the school, we must take into consideration the dual system of teachers and students, and

[12] Reprinted from Willard Waller, *The Sociology of Teaching* by permission of the publisher John Wiley & Sons, Inc. (Copyright 1932, Russell and Russell Inc.)

we must recognize that the two groups may not have identical norms and that the students are functioning in reference to the expectations of both the dominant teacher segment of the school society and those of their classmates and peers in the school society. In some situations, behavior in accord with the student expectations is required even though it may involve opposition to or avoidance of the expectations of teachers. Some have assumed that the students are the all-powerful reference group to which the individual refers himself for the evaluation of his behavior. Although this is a significant factor in understanding the behavior of students, to disregard the adult or teacher as a reference in the school system is unrealistic. As Waller notes, the teachers are and must be in control. There are many ways by which the students can avoid the performance of the behavior expected by teachers but the society assigns to the teachers the task of accomplishing certain ends with regard to the student's behavior. When these conflict with student's expectations, the achievement of the teacher's goals may be less than desired. The fact remains, however, that much of the behavior expected by the teachers is acquired in the school.

▶ *Adult and Student Expectations.* The impact of teachers' expectations on elementary students was demonstrated by Rosenthal and Jacobson.[13] Randomly selected students in 18 elementary classrooms were identified as likely "spurters" by researchers who had administered an intelligence test to all students. Subsequent tests revealed that the students whom the teachers had been told would improve had done so to a significantly greater extent than the students in the same classrooms who were not identified as "spurters." Apparently the expectations of teachers were fulfilled by increase in intelligence as well as school performance. The results of this study supports both the general hypothesis that students behave in terms of others' expectations and that teachers' expectations are relevant to elementary age students. The expectations of

[13] Robert Rosenthal and Lenore Jacobson, *Pygmalion in the Classroom,* (New York: Holt, Rinehart, 1968).

teachers as well as other adults and students affect the student's school performance.

Recent concern with adolescent society and emphasis on individualized instruction have caused many to overlook the norms and expectations held for students by teachers and other adults. Although the adult definitions of appropriate behavior vary somewhat from one school to another and for particular students, some commonalities are clearly present. For example, all school authorities and teachers expect essentially all of the children to learn basic reading, writing, and use basic arithmetic skills. Although there has been much criticism of the failure of schools to achieve their goals, it is clear that a high degree of success is attained in these areas. Nearly 100 per cent of the children who attend American schools learn these skills to a significant level. This is true in spite of the fact that we have wide acceptance of the theory of limited abilities which would indicate that some students could not learn these basic skills.

In addition to these basic skills, certain aspects of natural science, history of the nation, and various other areas of knowledge are considered important by nearly all teachers and other adults connected with the school. Although schools may differ somewhat on the knowledge they are expected to acquire in each, the teachers do set certain norms of skill and knowledge which they apply to essentially all students at various ages. The frequently expressed concern about a school's inadequacy or failures is evidence that these norms exist.

At the upper grade levels, the teachers and other adults differentiate extensively between the behavior expected of some students and that expected of others. This differentiation occurs to some degree in the early elementary grades but it becomes more pronounced in the secondary grades when the students are assigned to different curricula. Through the processes of differentiation, the students come to understand that the adult society as represented by the teachers and other school officials does not expect the same behavior of all students. Thus, the school provides alternate patterns of formal learning as the larger society does in other areas of behavior.

A particular alternate curriculum is not required of everybody and the specific areas of knowledge required of students enrolled in a given curriculum may vary considerably from time to time and from student to student. As we have noted earlier, one of the functions of the school is to classify and select students for particular kinds of learning and through this enabling them to assume various positions in society.

The norms of the society and the teacher's expectations reflect this function. Teachers generally feel that it is not appropriate for everyone to learn advanced mathematics and science or senior English which characterize most college preparatory curricula. Both the teachers and out-of-school adults believe it is quite appropriate for a significant proportion of the students to learn quite different types of knowledge and skill in the secondary school. This differentiation in function is highly valued and the quality of education provided by a school is currently rated in part on the range and variety of curriculum opportunities available. The secondary schools are seldom, if ever, rated on their success in teaching all students the same knowledge and behavior as the early elementary school is judged on its success in teaching all to read.

In addition to the formal curricula, there are many other types of behavior that are considered appropriate and are expected by the adult segment of the school group. Both boys and girls are expected to learn to behave in the appropriate manner for their sex. This and many other culturally required behaviors are taught in an informal manner by the teachers in every school. Although such subjects may not be specified in the course schedule, it is not difficult to identify a wide range of behaviors which teachers expect children and adolescents to acquire. We have thought of athletics as a student-valued behavior and we shall recognize it as such in the following section, but athletics are also very much a part of the adult culture in the United States. Both teachers and other adults constantly socialize the young people into this athletic complex. It is not surprising therefore that various types of athletic behavior have been introduced into the school in both the formal curricula and in extra curricular activities.

The emphasis on athletics in the secondary schools results from adult as well as student interest. In this instance the interests and values of the student and adult segments of the school society converge.

The contest and perhaps latent conflict between students and adults in the school tend to produce some student norms at variance with the norms held by adults in the school. This divergence may lead observers of the school culture to minimize the teachers' effectiveness in socializing students in the areas of behavior which teachers value. In emphasizing these failures, we have sometimes conveyed the impression that teachers' expectations are irrevelant to students and are ignored by them. Although many students would not identify teachers as significant others, few students fail to understand that certain types of behavior are expected of them and nearly all acquire a minimum level of the knowledge and skills expected by the teachers. Some observers have been so concerned about the norms of the student groups that they have ignored the extent to which students learn to behave as adults expect them. For example, Coleman states:

> A shock awaits the adult who makes his first venture into the present day world of adolescence. He finds it populated with jazzed-up autos, athletic stars, and "the group," that most powerful agent in a teenager's life, which calls him to go for a ride, or to go down to the snack bar, or just to come and "hang around."[14]

Coleman analyzed the value expectations of the high-school adolescents in part by identifying what the students considered necessary to get into the leading crowds in the high schools which he studied. He then answered the question, What does it take to get into the leading crowd in these schools?

> According to the adolescents themselves (and we asked all of them this question) it takes a lot of things; but academic success is not one of them. It takes athletic prowess, knowing how to dance, owning a car, having a good reputation, or liking to have fun. It takes being a good date, liking

[14] James S. Coleman, *Adolescent and the Schools*, pp. 18-19.

parties, and often not being a prude (for girls) or a sissy (for boys). Good grades and intelligence are mentioned, but not very often and not as often as any of the other items.[15]

In spite of the report that academic success is not valued, Coleman also indicates that all members of the leading crowds in the schools studied were college-bound students. This indicates that high-school students recognize that they must acquire certain kinds of behavior expected by adults including a degree of competence in the formally prescribed curriculum. The school dropouts and the poorer students who do not learn the prescribed patterns of behavior reasonably well are seldom in the leading crowds. The contest between the students and the teachers in the total institution tends to lead the students to minimize the importance of the adult-expected behavior, but the students do not ignore the teachers for they at least seek to achieve the minimum levels of performance acceptable to the adults.

It should be recognized also that the types of behavior identified by the students as essential for participating in the leading crowd are valued by adults as well. Athletic prowess, dancing, owning a car, having a good reputation, and acceptance by the opposite sex are quite as highly valued in adult society as they are in the student society. Failure to mention academic achievement may simply reflect the students' desire to avoid emphasizing the behavior constantly demanded by those who control the institution.

The norms of the high-school age reference groups may differ in some respects from those of the adult groups. The adolescent vocabulary, types of music desired, clothing styles, and a variety of other activities perceived as appropriate and expected by the adolescent crowd are in some degree divergent from those of the adults. It does not follow, however, that the adult expectations are irrelevant in the lives of the students. We maintain that children and youth in school learn to behave in terms of the expected behaviors associated with many roles.

[15] *Ibid.*, p. 19.

Both elementary and secondary school students come to behave in terms of the role expectations held by their parents, peers, and teachers, as well as many other persons and groups, whose expectations they value as important. The questions asked in some research in this field assume that the values of one group or another must take precedence in their effect on the student. For example, Coleman based much of his analysis of adolescent high-school society on forced choice questions such as this: "If you could be remembered here at school for one of the three things below, which one would you want it to be? "Brilliant student; athletic star; most popular."[16] In response to this forced-choice question, thirty-one per cent of the boys said brilliant student, forty-four per cent said athletic star and twenty-five per cent said most popular.[17] Although a larger proportion of the boys in the high schools studied gave athletic star preference over brilliant student, there is no evidence that they did not value both. Similar questions were asked of students in a large mid-western school system, but they were given the opportunity to indicate if they would like to be both a good student and a good athlete as well as one or the other. In the three high schools in the system, 87 per cent of the boys indicated that they would like to be known both as a good athlete and a good student.[18] Most of these boys do not consider academic success undesirable. Rather, doing well in academic work as well as athletics is valued highly by nearly all high-school boys. They may devalue behavior that emphasizes brilliance to the exclusion of any other kind of activity for the student who over-displays his brilliance is identified as a "square." This is further demonstrated by Tannenbaum's study of the acceptability of ascribed traits among high-school students. He asked the students to rate eight different types in order of acceptability with the following results:

[16] James S. Coleman, *The Adolescent Society, op. cit.*

[17] *Ibid.*, p. 134.

[18] This was part of a larger study by the authors and associates on Self-Concept of Ability and School Achievement. These data were analyzed by Nelson Goud.

[19] Abraham J. Tannenbaum, *Adolescents Attitudes Toward Academic Brilliance* (unpublished doctoral dissertation, New York University).

1. Brilliant, non-studious, athlete.
2. Average, non-studious, athlete.
3. Average, studious, athlete.
4. Brilliant, non-studious, non-athlete.
5. Brilliant, studious, athlete.
6. Average, non-studious, non-athlete.
7. Average, studious, non-athlete.
8. Brilliant, studious, non-athlete.

Athletes are rated higher as a whole than non-athletes, but it should also be noted that the brilliant student is rated higher than the average student when described as non-studious. The non-studious student is always rated above the studious one with brilliance and athletics controlled. This suggests that the characteristic most disliked is studiousness. We do not know exactly what this implies to high-school students, but it probably suggests a person with a limited range of interests and an exclusive concentration on study. The most acceptable person was the brilliant athlete who was not studious.

The general conclusion derived from these studies is that high-school students value both athletics and good academic performance. They do not, however, like their peers to display their studiousness. Perhaps they would also dislike athletes who displayed their "athleticness" constantly without other characteristics. The norms of the student group include a wide range of behavior. Some are strictly adolescent but other behaviors valued by students are also valued by teachers and parents. These norms include good academic performance if it is not displayed to the exclusion of the athletics or other activities which the adolescents also value.

Variation Between Schools and School Groups

Although there are some commonalities in the high-school culture and certainly in the adult expectations held for students, there is considerable variation in norms from one school to another and from one classroom to another. Studies of the curricula and the levels of achievement expected in various schools demonstrate quite clearly that school teachers, administrators, and students hold differing expectations of student performance in the various schools. This is reflected in the types of curricula that are provided for the students and in the norms of achievement considered appropriate by the teachers, students, and other relevant groups.

The variation in the academic norms of high-school teachers and students and the impact of the norms on school achievement and college plans has been demonstrated in a sample of twenty schools.[20] A six factor measure of school climate was developed from the reports of both students and teachers. The variance in these measures of academic and social norms of the school social systems accounted for a significant proportion of the variation in both mathematics achievement and college plans when individual factors such as abstract reasoning ability and family socio-economic status have been controlled.

The variation in the school achievement and other behavioral norms from one school to another are generally related to the social composition of the student body. Recent studies of social class and racial composition of schools reveal that both variables are related to school achievement and the attitudes of students.[21] Although other factors are involved, the higher achievement in schools with predominantly white middle-class students probably results in part from the higher norms for achievement in these schools. The study of school climates by McDill, Meyer, and Rigsby indicated that the variation in school norms was more highly related to academic

[20] Edward McDill, Edmund Meyers, Jr., and Leo Rigsby, *Source of Educational Climates in High School*, Final Report. Project No. 1999. U.S. Office of Ed. H.E.W. Baltimore, Dept. of Human Relations, Johns Hopkins University, 1966. Also McDill, Meyer and Rigsby, "Institutional Effects on Academic Behavior of High School Students." *Soc. of Ed.* 40:3 pp. 181-199, 1967.

[21] *See* James Coleman and others, *Equality of Educational Opportunity* U.S. Office of Education. National Center for Educational Statistics. Washington U.S. Government Printing Office, 1966. U.S Commission on Civil Rights, *Racial Isolation in the Public Schools.* Vol. I, Washington, D.C. U.S. Government Printing Office, 1967.

performance than the variation in the social class composition of the schools. Although the socio-economic composition is related to academic norms, some schools with fewer middle class students have relatively high achievement norms.[22]

Parents, as well as teachers and students in schools with predominantly white middle-class students, usually expect the students to perform well in the academic curriculum while the norms in most predominantly lower class and Negro schools define lower achievement as acceptable and appropriate. Exceptions to this generalization can be found but it is clear, as we will analyze further in Chapter 6, that both the social class composition and the racial composition are related to the variation in school norms and school achievement.

Although the entire social context of the school community affects the norms of performance and the expectations held for the students in different schools, the school faculty generally holds these differential expectations and probably communicates them to the students. In a sample of urban elementary schools, the principals of schools with the highest socio-economic status on the average expected 64 per cent of their pupils to go to college and only 7 per cent to drop out before they finished high school. In contrast, the principals of the elementary schools with the lowest socio-economic status expected only 7 per cent of their students to go to college and 44 per cent to drop out before they complete high school.[23] These differences in level of school attendance expected are almost certainly associated with differential levels of performance in the elementary schools.

Variation Within Schools

In addition to the difference in norms between schools, there are differences within a school society. Teachers and administrators, as well as students, have different expectations of the students enrolled in different curricula and of particular

[22] McDill, *et al.*, 1967, *op. cit.* pp. 195-196.
[23] Robert E. Herriot and Nancy Hoyt St. John, *Social Class and the Urban School* (New York: John Wiley & Sons, Inc., 1966) pp. 51-53.

classes taking the same courses. The whole system of curriculum variation and "ability grouping" within a given course or curriculum is a reflection of the differential role expectations which teachers hold for students in the different groups. Such classifications are generally based on the assumption that the students have fixed and varied abilities which are best accommodated by the differential curricula and groups. Regardless of the assumptions about ability, however, the assignment or guidance of students into various academic programs reflects the school's expectations with regard to their performance. The impact of the teachers' expectations on the child's measured ability is clearly demonstrated by Rosenthal and Jacobson.[24] Such effects are also translated into academic achievement.

In addition to the variations in academic expectations, the teachers and other school officials hold varied expectations for students in numerous other areas of behavior. It can be said that the expectations which teachers hold for particular students in most areas of behavior are different rather than similar. We should therefore characterize the faculty norms applied to students as alternate rather than common patterns of behavior. There are, of course, some exceptions to this generalization. Such common activities as attending class and wearing "appropriate" clothing are expected of all, but in general the faculty expects different types of academic and other behavior from different individuals.

Informal sub-groups within a student body also have varied norms of behavior. A number of studies of college and high-school students have identified different student subcultures. One of these distinguishes between the high-school "fun" sub-culture, the "academic" sub-culture, and the "delinquent" sub-culture.[25] As these names indicate, different subgroups in a high-school student body hold differential expectations and display different norms of behavior with

---

[24] Robert Rosenthal and Lenore Jacobson. *op. cit.*

[25] Burton Clark, *Educating the Expert Society* (San Francisco: Chandler Publishing Company, 1962). *Also see* Brookover *et. al. The College Student* (New York: 1964), Chapter by David Gottlieb.

regard to the various activities of the school. There are groups or segments of the student population in which high academic performance is considered appropriate and expected of the members. In other groups the norms of behavior are decidedly different.

In general, the behavior of students in a particular school will tend to be alike in those areas where there are universally applied norms and expectations. In other areas of behavior the differences in both the adult expectations and those of the student reference group will operate to produce differences in individual behavior.

IMPLICATIONS FOR EDUCATION

In line with our theoretical frame of reference, we would hypothesize that a relatively uniform high level of academic achievement could be accomplished if there were a universal and homogeneous set of expectations held by all significant others for all students in the school. Just as practically all children learn the common elements of the expected cultural behavior, they would learn the academic types of behavior such as algebra or science if all of the significant others and reference groups held uniformly high expectations for behavior in these areas. At the present time, it seems clear that many students are expected by their significant others to perform at low levels.

Certainly, most teachers and school authorities do not believe that all of their students should achieve at high levels, and in general, parents come to accept the expectations which teachers advocate.[26] We thus have a school community in which the significant others may all expect low levels of achievement from certain categories of students and particular individuals. A self-fulfilling prophecy of low-achieving students results.

In recent years, experiments have been designed to raise the academic performance of lower-class students. The Banneker program in St. Louis which attempts to persuade teach-

[26] See Brookover *et. al., Self-Concept of Ability and School Achievement III, op. cit.*

ers and parents, as well as students, to accept the idea that children in lower socio-economic disadvantaged categories can achieve well in school has succeeded in raising achievement to some degree. Although the Rosenthal and Jacobson experiments[27] suggest that changes in teachers' expectations result in increased achievement, other experiments with teachers and other school personnel have not always been as successful.

Attempts by the authors and their associates to change students' self-concepts of ability and achievement through counseling and a learning specialist were not effective in enhancing the students' conceptions of themselves or their performance.[28] When teachers and parents as well as other relevant groups were involved, changes in students were more easily observed.[29]

Since parents are significant others for nearly all students, chances of success in enhancing the achievement is greater if parents are included among the reference groups and significant others whose expectations for the students are enhanced. Experience with a small group of parents suggests that the modification of the expectations of parents alone may be effective in raising the achievement of their sons and daughters.[30] It seems likely, however, that changes in achievement are most likely to occur when all of the significant others including parents, teachers, and friends hold expectations for a higher level of performance.

The higher achievement of lower class and Negro students in predominantly white middle-class schools is evidence of the impact of higher levels of expectation by all segments of the social system.[31] Although some limited success may be achieved

[27] Rosenthal and Jacobson, *op. cit.*

[28] W. B. Brookover, Jean LePere, Don Hamachek, and Shailer Thomas, *Self-Concept of Ability and School Achievement II*, Bureau of Publication Service, Michigan State University, East Lansing, 1965.

[29] See Mildred Smith, "Reading for the Culturally Disadvantaged," *Educational Leadership*, Vol. 22 (March, 1965).

[30] See Brookover *et. al. Self-Concept of Ability and School Achievement II, op. cit.*

[31] *Equality of Educational Opportunity, op. cit.* and *Racial Isolation in the Public Schools, op. cit.*

by compensatory education programs for the disadvantaged, it is likely that most of these students will not attain high levels of achievement unless they are permitted to attend schools in which teachers, friends, and others in the school expect them, as well as "advantaged" students, to learn the valued academic behavior.

We postulate on the basis of the performance of students in schools and groups where uniformly high expectations are held that few children would fail to achieve adequate academic performance if such norms were universally held by all of the child's significant others. The present system in which all academic significant others hold low expectations for many students and the norms of the entire school system maintain that many students should not achieve at high levels is almost certain to perpetuate a low level of academic performance for large segments of the student population. Those students, for whom different significant others hold differing expectations, are likely to perform in accord with the expectations held by the significant others or group that is most important to the student. Changes in the expectations of the teachers, therefore, are unlikely to have significant impact unless the teacher is an important referent for the student.

The contemporary concern with the education of disadvantaged youngsters makes a consideration of this frame of reference extremely important. We are now asked to enhance the achievement of students we have previously identified as non-learners. It is unlikely that such changes in the school achievement will occur unless the norms of the school-community are modified so that all persons with whom the child interacts believe he can learn and consider high achievement appropriate for the disadvantaged as well as middle-class children.

In accord with our basic theory, we postulate that the types of behavior learned by students in school is affected by the expectations of the groups and significant others to whom the student refers in evaluating his own behavior. Therefore, an understanding of the differences as well as the similarities in behavior among students in part depends upon an identification of the reference groups and the significant others for the students and the expectations which these persons and groups hold for the student. We have sought in this chapter to examine the range of groups and persons to which the individual refers himself and to appraise the norms and behavioral expectations held by these reference groups and significant others.

Objective analysis of the relevant variables suggests a misinterpretation of the available data and that conclusions based upon unsubstantiated assumptions have been common. Certainly, the adolescent society and its norms of behavior are important variables in affecting the high-school student's behavior, but the assumption that parents and teachers expectations are irrelevant does not seem justified. Parents, generally, and teachers, frequently, are significant others to students at all elementary and secondary age levels. The expectations of these adults, as well as other people who may be significant in the lives of students, must therefore be considered in an analysis of the child's learning in school.

In a similar manner, many false conclusions have been drawn concerning the expectations held for students by various groups. Teachers and other school authorities frequently explain the low academic achievement of students by asserting that the parents and the peers do not value academic achievement. Although this may be true to some extent, there is little evidence to indicate that parents expect their sons and daughters to do poorly at the outset of their school careers. They may acquire such expectations as the child goes through the various grade levels. In the process of assigning responsibility to parents and peers, teachers seldom recognize that they hold different expectations for different groups of children. Since they operate on a theory of limited abilities and a strong belief in adapting curricula to individual differences, teachers generally hold different expectations for children in different schools and in different groups of students within the school. It is not uncommon for teachers and counselors to try to help a child acquire more realistic aspirations. This generally means that the child, and perhaps his parents, should lower their academic aspirations and expectations for the child.

It is not surprising that we have wide variations in the academic achievement of students in a school social system where all the significant others and reference groups hold widely varying expectations for students in different categories. These variations in expectations held by significant others and reference groups create a social environment in which vast differences in academic achievement is the norm.

This variation in the normative expectations with regard to achievement is common among both the adult and student segments of the educational social system. Although the students continually try to minimize the control of the faculty over their behavior, it should not be concluded that all teachers have uniformly high expectations for the academic behavior of the students and that the student society has low expectations in this area of behavior. Rather, the facts are that students value high academic performance so long as it is not accompanied with a display of studiousness and a rejection of the types of behavior valued. Similarly, teachers have varying expectations of students with regard to academic performance.

The achievement norms and expectations held for students vary from school to school and from one group of students to another. Differences in curricula and levels of academic emphasis are associated with such variation in norms. Both adults and student peers therefore expect quite different levels of school performance in different school groups. It is postulated that a more uniformly high level of school performance would be achieved if all significant others and groups held this expectation for all students.

SUGGESTED READINGS

BROOKOVER, WILBUR B., DAVID GOTTLIEB, IRVIN J. LEHMANN, ROBERT RICHARD, FRED J. THADEN, and ARTHUR M. VENER. *The College Student*. New York: The Center for Applied Research, 1965. A study of the college student, his values, beliefs, and career patterns, and changes in American values and educational practices.

CICOUREL, AARON V. and JOHN I. KITSUSE. *The Educational Decision Makers.* New York: The Bobbs-Merrill Company, Inc., 1968. An excellent study of how the social mechanisms and patterns of organization in a large urban high school affect the careers of students.

COLEMAN, JAMES. *Adolescent and the Schools.* New York: Basic Books, 1965. A summary of research findings on the influence of peers on school behavior.

DEWEY, RICHARD and W. J. HUMBER, *An Introduction to Social Psychology.* New York: The Macmillan Company, 1966, pp. 104-121. A very readable discussion of the concepts of significant others and reference groups.

RIESMAN, DAVID, *Constraint and Variety in Education.* New York: Anchor Books, 1958. Riesman describes the commonalities and differences in American schools and universities with reference to cultural and sub-cultural contexts.

5

The Self
in
Relation
to
Others

THROUGHOUT OUR DISCUSSION we have emphasized the need for new conceptions of school learning based on current knowledge. The traditional emphasis on fixed abilities as the major determinant of differences in learning is no longer in accord with the present state of scientific knowledge and the requirements of our social system. We need a conception of behavior which will allow us to account more successfully for variations in learning among students. More important, educational theory must provide us with the means for enhancing the achievement levels of the great majority of students to meet the demands of an increasingly complex technological society.

We have pointed out how variations in learning are associated with differences in cultural and sub-cultural experiences. We have seen how the cultural norms and the expectations and evaluations of others which are associated with social class, racial status, peer groups, families, and other social variables contribute to differences in educational attainment among students. Stated in its most elementary form, we know that people influence both what and how much individuals can and do learn.

Awareness that others influence learning leads to an important question. How do differences in academic achievement result from the views and actions of others with whom they interact? Obviously, for the acts of others to have an impact on one's behavior, that individual must perceive those acts. Perception of others, however, is so commonplace that it is easy to overlook important factors affecting this perception.

One important consideration is that the medium through which the views of others are transmitted and perceived is through the use of signs and symbols—primarily a shared language system. Many sociologists and social psychologists use the term "symbolic interaction" to emphasize that the basis of social behavior is communication. Social interaction is not merely a proximity of bodies. Social interaction involves for each participant an awareness of others. Each participant interprets and reinterprets the cues provided by those with whom he is interacting. More than that, it involves on the part of each interacting individual, an awareness and interpretation of self. This leads to a second feature of the social process.

As we develop a language we learn the labels or symbols to attach to our experiences. We learn what a chair is, what "no" means, what a hot stove implies, what a bad boy is, and so forth. We also learn to apply nouns, verbs, and adjectives to ourselves. We learn, in other words, to define ourselves in the same sense that we learn to define other persons and objects in our world. We define ourselves using the language systems of those with whom we come in contact. We should note that the development of language allows us to communicate with ourselves in much the same fashion as we communicate with others. Using the language we have acquired from others, we tell ourselves who we are, what is appropriate for us to do in this or that situation, what we have been, who we will be, and so forth. We question ourselves and we answer our own questions. *All of the attributes by which we characterize ourselves, all of the statements we make about ourselves, we refer to as the "self-concept structure."* It is this process of self-conceptualizing, the self-concept structure, which guides us in our decisions.

In the following discussion, we will further elaborate on what is meant by self-concept, the relevance of certain types of self-conceptions, and strategies for effecting changes in these self-conceptions and thereby effecting changes in academic behavior.

SELF-CONCEPTS IN RELATION TO ROLE

The idea of self-concept has probably been the subject of more concern among psychologists and sociologists than any other idea. Nearly every text on teaching and learning in the classroom for the past twenty years has given attention to the importance of self-concept in affecting an individual's behavior. The writings of Maslow,[1] Rogers,[2] and Combs and Snygg[3] have been perhaps the most influential sources of the educators' concern for the way in which individuals think of themselves. These and similarly oriented theorists have had an especially large impact on educational theory. This psychologically oriented tradition in education has tended to treat self-concept as a personal trait. Much like the concern in education for the measurement of each person's general intellectual capacity, independent of varying tasks, social conditions and experiences with others, educators have dealt with self-concept as if it were a trait like red hair. Most educators and psychologists speak of self-concept as if it were a unitary phenomenon within the individual and with a general applicability to rather disparate social conditions. Accordingly, it is not uncommon to hear educators speak of a student's low or high self-concept as if he held only one self-concept.

[1] Abraham H. Maslow, *Motivation and Personality* (New York: Harper & Brothers, 1954).

[2] Carl R. Rogers, *Client Centered Therapy* (Boston: Houghton Mifflin Co., 1951), pp. 481-532.

[3] Arthur W. Combs and Donald Snygg, *Individual Behavior* (New York: Harper & Brothers, 1959), pp. 16-37.

From our perspective, it is quite possible for a student to think of himself as handsome, a good dancer, popular, well liked, a good person, and yet as rather ignorant in statistics, a poor reader, and tired of school. No single summarizing statement of this individual's concept of self is appropriate. To think of this person as having a high, low, or average self-concept, in general, would ignore relevant characteristics of the student. Certain of these self-concepts will be more or less relevant depending on the social situation. If a student is faced with a problem in a statistics class, his self-concept as a poor statistics student is more likely to affect his achievement than is his self-concept as a good dancer. By the same token, a person may believe that others dislike him, that he is bad because he steals, and that he is very smart in mathematics. This person is likely to do better in math assignments than will students who think of themselves as "nice" guys but "dumb" in mathematics.

From the sociological perspective, the self-conceptions which are most relevant are those by which we define our role in the situation which we wish to account for.

In the previous chapters, we learned that there are culturally shared role expectations for each social position, for example, the roles of high-school history teacher, father, son, president of a bank, etc. While each individual learns that society, various groups, and certain persons expect him to behave in particular ways in each of his roles, he also develops role expectations for self which are a function of his unique experiences with others. Whatever these role expectations for self as a student, girl, and so forth are, they are by definition self-concepts.

We are primarily interested in those self-conceptions which define for individuals their roles as students. Some students may conceive of themselves in their reading roles as disliking reading while at the same time feel quite competent as readers. Some females may feel rejected by others yet feel that they would make someone a good housewife if someone would just marry them.

One other point about the relation between role and self-concept should be noted. Roles often indicate reciprocal relationships with others. For example, the role of father specifies behaviors with reference to the reciprocal roles of son or daughter under varying conditions, e.g. whether one ought to spank, whether one can spank, under which conditions to spank, and where to spank. Similarly, the role of teacher is defined with reference to students and vice versa. Restated, one's self-conceptions about his role as a student indicates to the individual whether he ought to learn certain things, where he can learn those things, and if so, when and where to learn them. Self-conceptions, therefore, vary with the situation. A student may feel quite able to read with his peers in class while also believing that he is unable to read in front of a large group of parents. Simply put, there is no one self-concept of reading ability or any other self-concept which is operative in all situations.

Values Placed on Roles for Self

For each role that we acquire we also learn to value that role in comparison with other roles. This value is a function of the extent to which we perceive that others will allow us to achieve or maintain desired social relationships as well as personal satisfactions. We learn what it will cost us if we violate the role requirements. We may learn that if we do certain things others will exclude us from relationships with them or that we will experience guilt. In a similar fashion, we learn to anticipate a sense of personal satisfaction or rewards from others at the thought of carrying out certain role performances. Some roles are more crucial to us than others in the sense that to violate one role is to affect many other roles.

Generally, educators stress the monetary, occupational, and social benefits which good students may attain in later life. Rather it appears as if many educators encourage the student to divorce his student role from his relationships with parents and friends. The coach, of course, is an exception with many more advantages than the typical teacher of academic subjects. When the coach rewards an individual by putting him on the team or praising his athletic ability, he has a major impact on many of the individual's relationships with peers, friends, family—in fact, the whole community.

In other words, the generalized impact of teachers on the many roles of the students is likely to be less than that of coaches. Some teachers attempt with varying amounts of success to get their students to believe that adequate performance in the role of the student will have a desired impact on their other roles. Fortunate is the teacher who has the support of parents, friends, or students in placing importance on the role of student.

An additional consideration is that many children may be viewed by their teachers as not benefiting from student achievement. Behavior reflected in such common phrases as: "why should these lower-class children take advanced work, they aren't going on to college anyway," or "these lower-class students need vocational preparation and not academic preparation," further tends toward the devaluation of the student role by these children.

Self-evaluation of ability to carry out a role also affects the value that students attach to that role. Some students are taught that they do not have the ability to successfully learn advanced skills and knowledge. As developed in the next section and in other chapters, society—and our schools in particular—spends considerable effort on convincing a large number of students that they are not academically capable. Such students must devalue their roles as students or else experience serious frustration. Efforts to get such students to value the role of high achiever are not likely to be very successful unless they learn that they have the ability to achieve at higher levels in school.

Self-Concept of Academic Ability

As indicated in Chapter 1, an individual's self-concept of academic ability is an important variable in the decisions he makes to carry out the role of student. In the United States, as well as in many other cultures, large numbers of students are academically impeded by low self-concept of academic ability. Self-concept of academic ability functions to set limits of achievement for many students. Self-concept of ability is a "threshold" variable. By this it is meant that a self-concept of ability is only a necessary, but not a sufficient condition for achievement—for example, if a person does not think he is able to learn an activity he will not organize his activities to learn; however, if he thinks he can learn he may still choose not to learn and direct his attention elsewhere.

This model for learning should not be interpreted to mean that biological differences—for example, those resulting from deafness or neurological impairment—play no part in achievement levels. Within the framework of organic states, emotional conditions, and previously developed skills, self-concepts of what is appropriate and possible also influence learning. Even such persons as those labeled "educable mentally retarded" may so learn that they cannot learn, that even under the most sophisticated special education activities, they are needlessly hindered in their learning.

Recent research by the authors and their associates shows that self-concept of academic ability is significantly correlated with school achievement. Self-concept accounts for a significant portion of achievement independent of measured intelligence, socio-economic status, educational aspirations, and the expectations of family, friends, and teachers.[4] In these longitudinal studies, following an entire class of students in a large midwestern city, from grades seven through twelve, changes in the self-concepts of academic ability of students were asso-

[4] Wilbur B. Brookover, Jean M. LePere, Don E. Hamachek, Thomas, Shailer and Edsel L. Erickson, *Self-Concept of Ability and School Achievement, II,* Educational Research Series, Number 31, Cooperative Research Project, Number 1636. Bureau of Educational Research Services, College of Education, Michigan State University, East Lansing, Michigan, October, 1965; Brookover, Wilbur B., Erickson, Edsel L., Joiner, Lee M., Educational Research Series, Number 36, Cooperative Research Project, Number 2831, February, 1967. *Self-Concept of Ability and School Achievement, III,* Educational Publication Services, College of Education, Michigan State University, East Lansing, Michigan.

ciated with changes in achievement level. In support of the idea that self-concept of academic ability is a threshold variable, studies showed that although a significant proportion of students with high self-concepts of ability achieved at a relatively lower level (approximately 50 per cent), practically none of the students with low self-concepts of ability achieved at a high level.

Confirmation that there is a strong association between self-concept of academic ability and academic achievement has also been shown in studies of mentally retarded children,[5] delinquent adolescents,[6] hearing and visually impaired students in schools for the deaf and blind,[7] and school dropouts.[8] Further experimental evidence is cited in the discussion on strategies for changing self-concepts of ability. All of the aforementioned research, along with a large number of other investigations,[9] suggests that a significant number of students are being needlessly hindered by low self-conceptions of academic ability. The importance of this state of affairs cannot be overemphasized at this time. Even the value placed on being a student is affected by self-concept of ability as a student. Therefore, strategies must be developed for enhancing the self-conceptions of ability for a large proportion of our students. Before we discuss these strategies, however, it is important to understand the relative impact of parents and teachers on students' self-concept of academic ability.

[5] Richard E. Towne, and Lee M. Joiner, *The Effect of Special Class Placement on the Self-Concept of Ability of the Educable Mentally Retarded Child Report* on U. S. Office of Education grant 32-32-0410-6001, Michigan.

[6] David Haarer, *A Comparative Study of Self-Concept of Ability Between Institutionalized Delinquent Boys and Non-Delinquent Boys Enrolled in Public Schools.* Unpublished Ph.D. Dissertation, Michigan State University, 1969.

[7] Lee M. Joiner, and Edsel L. Erickson, *Scales and Procedures for Assessing Social-Psychological Characteristics of Visually Impaired and Hearing Impaired Students,* U. S. Office of Education Cooperative Research Project No. 6-8720, Washington: U.S. Government Printing Office, 1967.

[8] Kenneth Harding, *A Comparative Study of Caucasian Male High School Students Who Stay in School and Those Who Drop Out.* Unpublished Ph.D. Dissertation, Michigan State University, 1969.

[9] Ruth C. Wylie, *The Self Concept* (Lincoln, Nebraska: University of Nebraska Press, 1961).

THE IMPACT OF PARENTS AND
TEACHERS ON SELF-CONCEPT

Basic to this discussion is the relation between students' self-concept and the evaluations of others. Table 3 illustrates how self-concept of academic ability is dependent on perceptions of others. The previously mentioned six-year study of 561 public school students, from grades seven through twelve, revealed that perceived parental evaluations were more highly correlated with students' self-concept of academic ability than were students' perception of teachers' evaluations.[10] This is in accord with the findings cited in Chapter 4, which indicated parents of public school children are more likely to be academic significant others to their children than are the children's teachers.

We must be cautious, however, in drawing conclusions about what is or what can be the impact of teachers on students' self-concept. In other research it was found[11] that among institutionalized students self-concept was much more dependent on teachers' evaluations than it was among non-impaired children. In fact, the teachers of deaf institutionalized children were concluded to be equally if not more important than parents in affecting students' self-concept of academic ability. There are a number of possible reasons for this: (1) Parents of children who are profoundly or severely deaf are likely to be more limited in their ability to communicate with their children than are teachers of the deaf. (2) Teachers of deaf children are likely to be perceived as more authoritative and credible by both parents and students than are teachers in the public schools. (3) Teachers in institutions for the deaf have more occasion to reinforce their beliefs with students. (4) In institutions for impaired children the role of student is closely related to the many other roles played. In fact, often the grouping of such children as to type of student is the basis for living assignments, civic responsibilities,

[10] See footnote 4 above.
[11] Joiner and Erickson, *op. cit.*

TABLE 3

Perceptions of Others and Self-Conceptions as Intervening Variables
Between the Evaluations and Expectations of Others and School Performance

Evaluations and expectations held for student by others.	→	Student's perceptions of the evaluations and expectations held for them by significant others.	→	Student's evaluations and expectations of self.	→	Student's behavior.
e.g. Parents think John is of average ability, that he ought to mind his teacher, that he ought to learn to read, that "C's" are sufficient for him, that being a high achieving student is not as important as being a good athlete, etc. Friends do not care how well John does in school as long as he does not brag.		e.g. John thinks that his parents do not think he is brilliant but neither do they think he is dumb. He thinks Miss Jones, his history teacher, does not like sports, but he does not care. He thinks all the kids will like him better if he makes the team and so will his parents and Uncle Jim, whom John especially likes.		e.g. John thinks he can pass all of his subjects and maybe go on to college. "A's," however, are out of range. He thinks it is important not to cross the teacher and to study enough to meet the requirements for passing and staying on the team. John values making the team, being a friend, and being a nephew. John values being a student only for its instrumental functions.		e.g. John chooses to go out for sports, read only as required, studies enough to earn passing grades.

career opportunities, and friendships. The teacher in an institution for the impaired functions in many ways like the parent of the typical public school child. The teacher in the typical public or private school, on the other hand, may be limited in her ability to directly affect her children's self-concept of ability. Indirectly, however, this teacher has an impact of which she if often unaware. That is, a teacher is often the source of a parent's attitude toward his child's academic ability. Teachers by their communications to parents probably have a great impact on students' self-concept of ability. More will be said about this in the section on strategies.

Strategies for Enhancing Self-Concept

How may we effectively bring about desired changes in the self-concepts of students? It is one thing to determine factors which are important in the development of self-conceptions, it is quite another to bring those factors into play. Sometimes the consequences of our planning are not anticipated. The following anecdote which was summarized in the *American Journal of Sociology*[12] illustrates this point:

A group of graduate students in a seminar in social psychology became interested in the notions implied in the interactionist approach. One evening after the seminar, five of the male members of the group were discussing some of the implications of the theory and came to the realization that it might be possible to invent a situation where the "others" systematically manipulated their responses to another person thereby changing that person's self-concept and in turn his behavior. They thought of an experiment to test the notions they were dealing with. They chose as their subject (victim) the one girl in their seminar. The subject can be described as, at best, a very plain girl who seemed to fit the stereotype (usually erroneous) that many have of graduate student females. The boys' plan was to

[12] Reprinted from John W. Kinch, "A Formalized Theory of the Self-Concept," *The American Journal of Sociology*, LXVII (Jan. 1963) pp. 482-483, by permission of the University of Chicago Press (Copyright 1963, University of Chicago).

begin in concert to respond to the girl as if she were the best-looking girl on campus. They agreed to work into it naturally so that she would not be aware of what they were up to. They drew lots to see who would be the first to date her. The loser, under the pressure of the others, asked her to go out. Although he found the situation quite unpleasant, he was a good actor and by continually saying to himself 'she's beautiful, she's beautiful . . .' he got through the evening. According to the agreement it was now the second man's turn and so it went. The dates were reinforced by the similar responses in all contacts the men had with the girl. In a matter of a few short weeks the results began to show. At first it was simply a matter of more care in her appearance; her hair was combed more often and her dresses were more neatly pressed, and before long she had been to the beauty parlor to have her hair styled, and was spending her hard earned money on the latest fashions in women's campus wear. By the time the fourth man was taking his turn dating the young lady, the job that had once been undesirable was now quite a pleasant task. And when the last man in the conspiracy asked her out, he was informed that she was pretty well booked up for some time in the future. It seems there were more desirable males around than those 'plain' graduate students.

Recently the authors and their associates conducted three one-year experimental studies.[13] Each experiment was designed to test a specific strategy for enhancing low-achieving students' self-concept of academic ability and thereby result in an increase in their academic achievement. One experiment involved working with parents, a second, a counselor, and another provided information to students in classroom settings by an "expert" from the university. The parental experiment was designed to enhance the academic expectations and evaluations parents held for their children's ability. The counseling experiment was designed to counteract the effects of parents who held low evaluations of their children's ability by having the counselor communicate high evaluations of academic ability to the students. The third experiment introduced an "expert"

[13] Brookover, LePere, Hamachek, Thomas and Erickson, 1965, *op. cit.*

from a university who presented to the students, directly and formally in classroom situations, information that they were academically able and that they ought to achieve at higher levels.

These experiments provided several insights. The only experiment which proved successful involved working with parents. In this experiment the parents were told not to reward or reinforce any negative statements their children might make about their academic ability. They were told to avoid even such statements as "Uncle Joe wasn't good in arithmetic either." The children were to be constantly told in subtle fashion that they were able and ought to do better in school. Any positive statement of ability by the student or any success in school was to be rewarded with commendatory remarks and support. The parents were told that small gains would occur and to make small but increasingly higher demands on the student.

Interestingly, as far as could be determined by the investigators, neither the students nor their teachers were made aware that an experiment was being conducted. The parents were told to avoid letting their children know that they were the topics of conversation. The parents, as far as the students were apparently aware, were merely meeting at the university to discuss general school-community problems.

Perhaps a key to the success of this experiment was that parents were told in the beginning that they were in part responsible for their children's low self-concept of academic ability and poor performance in school. The parents were told, however, that they could increase their children's self-concept of ability which in turn would lead to greater school achievement. While hostile at first to the thought of responsibility for their children's low achievement in school, the parents continued in the experiment, apparently motivated by the thought that possibly their children would improve and that they would feel guilty if they did not give the experiment a trial. After a few months when improvement was noted in the children, the parents reversed their feelings and became quite enthusiastic about the meetings and many sought further advice on strategies for eliciting change in their children's self-concept of academic ability. At the end of the school year when the experiment was stopped the parents sought to have it continued. The parents had changed to more positive attitudes toward their children's teachers, the role of the school, and an acceptance of their own role in affecting self-conceptions and achievements of their children.

The researchers, of course, used the same general techniques with the parents as they had taught the parents to use with their children. Recordings of group and individual sessions with parents indicate that the researchers emphasized the use of reward in the form of approval whenever a parent gave a desired response. A negative statement by a parent was ignored or given negative reinforcement. The researchers always treated the parents with a great deal of respect. They never, however, assumed any other stance than that responsibility for students' self-concept and achievement rested with the parents.

Unfortunately, the counseling experiment and the "expert" experiment did not result in changing the self-concepts of students or their performance in school. While these experiments differed in setting from each other and from the parent experiment, thus making comparisons difficult, it appears that the credibility of parents, friends, and teachers is greater than can be expected of a counselor or "expert" from the university. Apparently it is more effective to work through those who already have credibility and are significant others in the lives of students than it is to work directly with students.

Although there are many gaps in substantive knowledge about all of the variables affecting self-concept of ability, there is sufficient evidence to make a number of conclusions and recommendations. The first is that self-conceptions not only change, but that they can be changed in positive directions. The second is that simply having anyone tell a student with a low self-concept of ability that he is able is not likely to produce results. Prior achievement is also of limited power. Students can often excuse their past performance. The reaction of certain others, however, to the performance of students seems to be quite important.

To be maximally efficient, a strategy to change the self-concepts of students' ability should involve those individuals who are already significant others. This means affecting the way that parents, friends, and teachers act toward the students. Perhaps a program to affect parental attitudes and reactions is as important as any classroom activity. The teachers ought not to be left out, however. In fact, the actions of teachers may well serve as a basis for parental judgments of their children's ability. The communication between teachers and parents of low-achieving students is commonly concerned with the faults in the children. Seldom are teachers able to communicate to the parents specific strategies for effecting changes in their children.

Furthermore, as previously discussed, the teacher and school often contribute to poor self-evaluations and performance by labeling children as "slow" through their manner of diagnosing and tracking students. Low achievement is too often excuse enough for providing inferior education, which in turn results in even lower achievement. Seldom are these vicious cycles broken.

SUGGESTED READINGS

BROOKOVER, WILBUR B., EDSEL L. ERICKSON, and LEE JOINER. *Self-Concept and School Achievement, III*, East Lansing, Michigan: Educational Publication Services, Michigan State University, 1967. Chapter I provides a critical review of research on the relationship between self-concept and achievement.

GORDON, CHAD and KENNETH J. GERGEN (eds.) *The Self in Social Interaction.* New York: John Wiley and Sons, Inc., 1968. Presents the main classic and contemporary perspectives of self-concept.

KINCH, JOHN W. "A Formalized Theory of the Self-Concept," *The American Journal of Sociology*, XVIII (1963), pp. 481-486.

LINDESMITH, ALFRED R. and ANSELM L. STRAUSS, *Social Psychology*, 3rd Edition. New York: Holt, Rinehart and Winston, 1968, Chapter XIV, "Selves and Roles," pp. 314-344. A very readable discussion of the nature and function of self-concept behavior.

MANIS, JEROME and BERNARD MELTZER (eds.) *Symbolic Interaction: A Reader in Social Psychology*. Boston: Allyn and Bacon, 1967. For the advanced student this is an excellent overview of symbolic interactionism.

6

Race
Class
and
Education

THE RELATION of education to racial and social class stratification of American society presents a timely illustration of the issues and ideas discussed in previous chapters of this book. Both educational policy issues and the social context of student performance in school, which we have discussed, have particular relevance for an analysis of racial and social class differences in educational programs. As we noted in Chapter 3, both the social class strata and the Negro minority have characteristics of sub-societies or sub-cultures in the larger society. The lower class strata, and particularly the minority group segments, are now the subject of major educational policy determination. This contemporary emphasis on the education of the disadvantaged makes the relation of racial and social class differences to educational policy and school performance an appropriate topic for analysis in this chapter.

SEGREGATION VS. EQUALITY OF OPPORTUNITY
IN AMERICAN EDUCATION

The American dilemma concerning racial segregation and equality of opportunity has characterized the educational system as well as other aspects of American society.[1] The segregation of Negroes in schools and residential areas is perhaps the most salient contemporary problem in American society. The vast majority of American Negroes is enrolled in completely segregated or predominantly Negro schools.[2] Development of the segregated schools for Negroes occurred in spite of our belief in equality of opportunity which has been highly cherished by nearly all Americans. During the nineteenth century, the common schools were organized to facilitate the achievement of this equality of opportunity goal. The social policy of a common educational experience for all students was reflected in the common school system. During the latter part of the nineteenth century, however, separate schools for Negroes were established in the South and in many Northern states. This deviation in the common school program was given legal sanction by the Separate-But-Equal-Doctrine approved by the U. S. Supreme Court in the Plessy-Ferguson decision in 1896. The rapid expansion of secondary schools and industrialization of society in the early decades of the twentieth century gave rise to the development of differentiated curricula and separate vocational and academic high schools for many whites as well as for Negro students. During the past century, therefore, we have seen the development of incompatible points of view and educational programs reflecting those points of view. On the one hand, the maintenance of a school system which would provide a common education for all Americans and through this a maximization of equality of opportunity; on the other hand, a segregated educational system which provides differentiated and unequal education for varying segments of the society.

[1] Gunnar Myrdal, *An American Dilemma* (New York: Harper and Brothers, 1944).

[2] James Coleman, *et. al.*, *Equality of Educational Opportunity*, Survey by United States Office of Education, Government Printing Office, 1966.

Until recently social and educational policy in America has been to maintain divergent racial sub-societies or castes. For a period following the freeing of the slaves, there was some confusion in public and educational policy but in the later decades of the nineteenth century the mores, the statutes, and court decisions clearly defined a segregation and separation policy. While large immigrant ethnic populations were being assimilated, the patterns of segregation and separation of the Negro and white sub-societies were solidifying. Although the United States drastically restricted immigration of some ethnic groups, the immigrant populations were generally considered appropriate inputs for assimilation into American society. However, the whites generally perceived Negroes as inferior to whites and therefore inappropriate for assimilation into the dominant white American society. The assumption of inferiority and the desire to maintain a subservient social stratum provided the basis for discrimination and a segregated sub-society. The educational system was designed to support and maintain the racial class system. Throughout the South, where most of the Negro population lived and in several Northern states, to which significant numbers of Negroes migrated, segregated schools were established for the Negro population.

For several decades, educators justified segregated schools on the assumption that the learning ability of Negroes was different from that of whites. This difference assumed both less ability among Negroes and differences in the kinds of behavior that whites and blacks could learn. The presumed difference is well illustrated by the belief commonly held among physical education teachers and coaches a few decades ago that Negroes could not run as fast as whites or Mongoloids because of the anatomical structures of their feet. Coaches, therefore, did not try to train Negro students for the dashes or sports requiring speed. Contemporary record holders demonstrate the falsity of such beliefs. Likewise, educators believed that Negroes generally were less able than whites to learn the academic subjects. This became the rationalization for providing a differentiated and, in many cases, inferior education for Negro students. Such inferior education assured that the Negroes would be chained to the unskilled and lower-stratum occupations which did not require academic preparation.

The doctrine of the common school, however, prevailed to some extent in the segregated school system. Negro children were taught some reading, writing, and arithmetic skills. Although they were not expected to achieve the same level of proficiency, when given the opportunity many Negro children not only learned to read but also learned the ideals of equality expressed in the Declaration of Independence, the Constitution of the United States, and other documents. The separate Negro schools, therefore, became vehicles through which the Negro sub-society acquired beliefs similar to those of whites concerning the goals of white American society. They then questioned why opportunities to achieve such goals were available to whites and not to Negroes in the segregated strata.

The knowledge and aspirations acquired by Negroes and many white Americans' guilt over the failure to provide equal opportunity to Negroes caused both to challenge the separate Negro society. The schools, therefore, serve both to maintain the segregated society and to provide the knowledge and attitudes which undermine its foundation.

The continuing conflict in American education between equality of opportunity and the differentiated segregated system of education has required many educators to find some basis for justifying the incompatible goals. The assignment of children to different and unequal educational programs at all levels—elementary, secondary, and higher education—has been justified on the basis of assumed differences in ability to learn and the society's needs for personnel with varied competence. Although such programs were hardly in harmony with equality of educational opportunity, many have argued that adjusting education to individual differences provides equal educational opportunity. A separate curriculum or track, as well as a segregated school for blacks or lower class people, has been justified on the assumption that this is the type of education that best meets the needs of those who are assigned there. On this basis, many have rationalized the allocation of large segments of the student body to differentiated educational programs as the best means of providing them equal opportunity. Although few educators maintain that disadvantaged groups on the whole have inferior ability, many types of ability grouping, tracking, and curricula serve to increase the relative disadvantage of Negro and other lower class children. The full range of differentiated educational programs for students whose social-cultural experiences result in different academic aptitude and achievement test scores is now being seriously questioned, and equality of educational opportunity is demanded for the disadvantaged segments of the society.

TYPES OF SCHOOL SEGREGATION

Before examining the recent changes in public policy and the constitutional foundations for the desegregation of education, we should delineate the methods of segregation. There are four general types of school segregation. The first of these is segregation by law or *de jure*; this is the segregation that has been required or permitted by the laws of the states or other political units. The legality of such segregation was attacked in the series of cases leading up to the *Brown* v. *Topeka Board of Education* decision of the Supreme Court in 1954. This decision struck down all legally prescribed segregated schools as unconstitutional because such schools denied equal protection of the law to those required to attend them.

The second type is commonly identified as *de facto*; this is the segregation of students which occurs as the result of residential patterns or other phenomena which produce segregated schools within a school district without legal prescription. A series of cases and state laws have focused on the question of *de facto* segregation.[3] It is now clear that it is unconstitutional to intentionally structure attendance areas within

---

[3] *See* J. Skelly Wright, "Public School Desegregation: Legal Remedies and Defacto Segregation," and Robert Carter, "De Facto School Segregation: An Examination of the Legal and Constitutional Questions Presented," in *Western Law Review*, Vol. 16, No. 3 (May 1965), pp. 478-531.

school districts to maintain segregation. The question of whether or not a state can be and should be controlled by law to correct purely *de facto* segregation in schools has not been finally decided by the courts. In a U.S. District Court decision, Judge J. Skelly Wright has held that racial or socio-economic *de facto* segregation through neighborhood schools or allied means denies the "Negro and poor public school children of their right to equal educational opportunity with the districts' white and more affluent public school children."[4] This and other lower court decisions have maintained that schools should take positive action to eliminate *de facto* segregation. If upheld by higher court, these decisions will require school systems to provide reasonable equality of educational opportunity to all racial and social class groups.

The third type of segregation has not been clearly specified in legal terminology, but it is clear that Negro and other disadvantaged students are frequently assigned to different curricula or tracks in the same or different schools.[5] Thus, the traditional vocational high schools are generally heavily imbalanced in racial and social class composition. Vocational or other non-college curricula in comprehensive high schools are generally provided for predominantly lower class and minority group students. Various types of tracking or ability grouping provide similar patterns of differentiated education. Assignment to groups or tracks, as well as some curricula, has generally been based on some criteria of presumably fixed ability or capacity to learn. The aptitude tests or other criteria generally reflect the disadvantages of lower classes and Negro sub-societies. By placement in less adequate educational programs the disadvantages of these students are exacerbated rather than reduced. The widely publicized track system developed in the District of Columbia schools was also condemned by Judge Wright as a denial of equality of educational oppor-

[4] Julius W. Hobson v. Carl Hansen, Supt. of Schools and The Board of Education of the District of Columbia. United States District Court for District of Columbia Civil Action No. 82-66, 1967.

[5] See Carl Hansen, *Four Track Curriculum for Today's High Schools*, (New York: Prentice-Hall, 1964) and Paul Woodring, *A Fourth of a Nation* (New York: McGraw Hill, 1957).

tunity and thus equal protection of the law in the 1967 United States District Court opinion.[6]

The fourth type of school segregation results from the organization of school districts. School districts' boundaries frequently separate the children of suburban middle and upper class whites from the lower class and Negro population of the central city. The quality of education provided in the suburban district is frequently superior to that in the central city by any acceptable criteria. The school districts therefore provide unequal education and their boundaries maintain the segregated system.

Such segregation and inequality has not yet been officially brought before a court for determination of its constitutionality, but Judge Wright has implied that school district organizations that provide unequal educational opportunities may be a denial of equal protection of the laws.[7]

RECENT CHANGES IN SEGREGATION POLICY

In the past three or four decades, we have witnessed significant changes in public policy concerning segregation of the schools. These changes are reflected in a series of court decisions as well as in state and federal legislation. A brief analysis of the steps in this process as reflected in the court decisions is appropriate.

Equal protection of the laws was guaranteed to all citizens by the 14th Amendment during the post-Civil War period. Some legislation and other actions initiated the implementation of this social policy in the first decades following the war. A reversal in policy followed and segregation was established by both legislation and court decisions in the late nineteenth century. The constitutional foundation for separate and differentiated education was not seriously questioned until about 1930. The first court challenges to the legal separation and differentiation in education for Negroes concerned professional and higher education. These cases challenged the fact that

---

[6] Hobson v. Hansen, *op. cit.*

[7] J. Skelly Wright, 1965, *op. cit.* and Hobson v. Hansen, 1967, *op. cit.*

Negroes were simply not admitted to southern graduate and professional schools and were not provided adequate facilities for such education in these states. The theory of differentiated ability on which much of the segregated and differentiated education is justified was firmly established in American educational beliefs and was not contested in the early Negro segregation cases. Neither was the contention that adequate and equal education might be provided in separate facilities. The United States Supreme Court decision in 1954 signaled a major change in the education policy by holding that segregated Negro schools could not be equal to schools for white children. In the *Brown* v. *Topeka Board of Education* decision, Chief Justice Warren stated that issue as follows:

> We come then to the question presented: Does segregation of children in public schools solely on the basis of race, even though the physical facilities and other 'tangible' factors may be equal, deprive the children of the minority group of equal educational opportunities? We believe that it does . . . The effect of this separation of educational opportunities was well stated by a finding in the Kansas case by a court which nevertheless felt compelled to rule against the Negro plaintiffs: 'Segregation of white and colored children in public schools has a detrimental effect upon the colored children. The impact is greater when it has the sanction of the law; for the policy of separating the races is usually interpreted as denoting the inferiority of the Negro group. A sense of inferiority affects the motivation of a child to learn. Segregation with the sanction of law, therefore, has a tendency to [retard] the educational and mental development of Negro children and to deprive them of some of the benefits they would receive in a racially integrated system.'[8]

Since 1954 many court and legislative acts have refined and extended national policy with regard to school segregation. Some courts have held *de facto* segregation or racially imbalanced schools acceptable unless it was shown to be intentionally designed by the responsible public officials. Other

[8] Brown and Topeka Board of Education, U. S. Supreme Court, 1954.

courts have ruled the racially imbalanced school a denial of equal opportunity. Although the U. S. Supreme Court has not yet acted on such a case, its refusal to review lower court cases which ordered positive action to correct *de facto* segregation or imbalance leaves such orders in effect in some cases. Judge Sweany's finding in the Barksdale case in Springfield, Massachusetts clearly states the basis on which he declared imbalance unconstitutional.

> The defendants argue, nevertheless, that there is no constitutional mandate to remedy racial imbalance. . . . but that is not the question. The question is whether there is a constitutional duty to provide equal educational opportunity for all children within the system. While Brown answered the question affirmatively in the context of coerced segregation, the constitutional fact—the inadequacy of segregated education—is the same in this case, and I so find. It is neither just nor sensible to prescribe segregation having its base in affirmative state action while at the same time failing to provide a remedy for segregation which grows out of discrimination in housing, or other economic or social factors. Education is tax supported and compulsory, and public school educators, therefore, must deal with inadequacies within the educational system as they arise, and it matters not that the inadequacies are not of their making. This is not to imply that the neighborhood school policy per se is unconstitutional, but that it must be abandoned or modified when it results in segregation in fact.[9]

It is clear from this finding that the courts were dealing with the issue of the inequality of education provided for some segments of the school population as well as racial segregation. The legal issue involved in both segregation and other unequal educational programs was clearly stated by Wright.

> The touchstone in determining equal protection of the law in public education is equal educational opportunity, not race. If classification by race is used to achieve the invidious discrimination, the Constitutional insult is exacerbated.

[9] Barksdale v. Springfield School Comm., 237 F. Supp. 543 (D Mass. 1965) at 546, also quoted by Wright 1965, *op. cit.* pp. 494-495.

But the focus must remain on the result achieved. If the ontoward result derives from racial classification, such classification is per se unconstitutional. For the result is segregation, and therefore unequal educational opportunity, the classification used whatever it is, is constitutionally suspect and a heavy burden is placed on the school board and the state to show, not only innocent intent, but also lack of suitable alternative. In short, since segregation in public schools and unequal educational opportunity are two sides of the same coin, the state, in order to provide equal educational opportunity, has the affirmative constitutional obligation to eliminate segregation however it arises.[10]

Judge Wright's 1965 statement clearly indicates that segregation and unequal educational opportunity cannot be separated. Any educational system that provides an inferior quality of education for any group of children for whatever reason is perceived as a denial of equal educational opportunity and therefore unconstitutional. After a thorough analysis of the track system in the District of Columbia Schools, Judge Wright concluded:

Even in concept the track system is undemocratic and discriminatory. Its creator admits it is designed to prepare some children for white-collar, and other children for blue-collar, jobs. Considering the tests used to determine which children should receive the blue-collar special, and which the white, the danger of children completing their education wearing the wrong collar is far too great for this democracy to tolerate. Moreover, any system of ability grouping which, through failure to include and implement the concept of compensatory education for the disadvantaged child or otherwise, fails in fact to bring the great majority of children into the mainstream of public education denies the children excluded equal educational opportunity and thus encounters the constitutional bar.[11]

Although Judge Wright's decision is based on only the Washington school program, the findings seem applicable to many grouping and tracking practices in other school systems.

[10] J. Skelly Wright, 1965, *op. cit.*, p. 494.
[11] Hobson v. Hanson, 1967, *op. cit.*, p. 177.

If this opinion or a similar one is upheld by the Supreme Court, any system of tracking or ability grouping based on presumed differences in capacities to learn, racial classification, or socio-economic levels will be unconstitutional. Special programs designed to overcome handicaps and compensate for disadvantages would likely be excepted. But evidence will be required to show that such remedial programs are remedial and not restricted opportunity programs to which disadvantaged students are assigned. In the light of Wright's decision, the doctrine that a limited capacity to learn can be determined by contemporary testing and observation methods and provide the valid basis for assignment to an unequal educational program will be difficult to sustain in the courts.

Many school districts developed voluntary attendance policies in which students were permitted to choose, at various stages, which schools they wished to attend. Such policies transferred the integration decisions to the students or their families who were generally influenced by local tradition and public opinion to continue segregated attendance where it existed. The Supreme Court has ruled in two cases[12] that freedom of choice plans alone are not sufficient to end school segregation in districts where previous state laws had required segregation. In such districts, school boards have an affirmative duty to eliminate discrimination by converting to a unitary system.

Although the Supreme Court decisions on freedom of choice were limited to states which previously required segregation, a Federal district court has ordered similar action in *de facto* segregation cases under the Civil Rights Act. In ordering the closing of predominantly Negro schools in an Illinois school district the Judge commented, "School boards and school administrators have a moral and civic duty as well as a legal duty to end segregation. To fail the Negro child would be to fail the nation."[13] Such court actions initiate a policy

[12] Green v. New Kent County School Board, and Moore v. Board of School Commissioners.

[13] Judge Julius Hoffman, in U. S. District Court No. District of Illinois Eastern Division, Plaintiff vs. School District 151 of Cook County, Illinois.

requiring positive action to eliminate discrimination and in-equality as well as barring actions which extend or continue segregation.

These court decisions are indicative of a new national policy on segregated and differentiated education in the United States. The various civil rights acts and the Office of Education guidelines, developed for the enforcement of the acts, have added further provisions for any school district receiving Fed-eral funds. Several states have passed legislation or initiated policies which stimulate school districts to take positive action to eliminate segregation and unequal educational opportunity. The process of change in educational policy and practice in the field will likely continue for some years. In fact, Federal support is being provided for separate vocational schools which seem as much a denial of equal opportunity as a tracking sys-tem. The specific details of the future laws and policies cannot yet be determined, but the general direction seems clear. Edu-cational programs differing in quality and providing inequality of opportunity for various segments of the student population will be seriously questioned. Schools providing differential programs will have to demonstrate that they serve to compen-sate for disadvantages or that the selection of students for different programs are based on valid criteria. Current methods of differential assignment based on tests with evident culture bias and low predictive validity will probably not be sustained if challenged in the courts.

The evolution, or perhaps more appropriately revolution, in educational policy regarding differentiated education reflects a change in our conception of equal educational opportunity.[14] Earlier, equal opportunity meant the provision of some mini-mum schooling for all students. Later, different programs for different children destined for different careers was the domi-nant concept. The 1954 decision, however, established that equal opportunity could not be provided in racially segregated schools. More recently, the outcome of the school program has become a major criterion of equality of educational oppor-

[14] *See* James Coleman, "The Concept of Equality of Educational Oppor-tunity," *Harvard Educational Review*, 38: 7-22 (Winter 1968).

tunity. It is essential therefore that we examine the effects of various types of school segregation on the performance of students.

THE EFFECTS OF SEGREGATION

Although segregated education is unequal education, the nature of the inequality and the effect of such education on its students have not been fully specified. The effects of segregated, racially mixed, or integrated schools on the personality or the academic achievement of children are not readily isolated from the effects of other social factors. The segregated schools are a part of a total social system and the effect of the particular segregation is very likely to depend on the way it is defined in the total social context and its relation to other aspects of social differentiation and stratification in the society. Differences that occur in the behavior of children in segregated schools of any sort are therefore the product of a whole complex of cultural differences. The school program is only one of the several differences between the disadvantaged and other strata which produce different behavior. The varied norms of appropriate behavior in the sub-culture, socialization in the family and neighborhood, the limited access to jobs and housing, are associated with the performance of lower class and black children in school as well as their behavior in other roles. It is therefore difficult to isolate the effects of various types of segregated school organization on student achievement, but the design of quality educational programs for the disadvantaged depends on knowledge of the effect of various school organizations.

Analysis of the effects of segregation involves both the identification of the effects on student behavior and the identification of the factors in school that produce that behavior. If possible, the impact of school factors must be separated from the impact of all other forces affecting the students' behavior. Although significant research has been completed in this field, conclusions regarding the precise effect of segregated or integrated schools are not yet definitive.

The *Brown* v. *Topeka Board of Education* decision which drew upon the social science knowledge available at the time has generally been substantiated by subsequent research. A recent survey by the U. S. Office of Education authorized under the Civil Rights Act of 1964[15] and further analysis of that and other research by the U. S. Commission of Civil Rights[16] confirms the 1954 position that Negro students do better in predominantly white schools than in segregated Negro schools. Although racial composition of the school affects the performance of Negro students, the students' family background and social class composition of the school also contribute to the students' behavior in schools. The contribution of racial and social class composition of the school-to-school performance and attitudes as well as out-of-school behavior were analyzed by both the U. S. Office and the Commission on Civil Rights. From its analysis of the process by which the achievement of students, particularly lower class ones, are affected by the social class composition of the student body, the U. S. Commission on Civil Rights concluded as follows:

It is difficult to specify precisely the ways in which the student environment affects performance and attitudes. There is a complicated relationship between the standards set by the performance and attitudes of a student's schoolmates and his own performance and attitudes. It seems reasonable to suggest, however, that at least two elements are present.

First, different backgrounds influence what students see as attainable goals. A disadvantaged student in school mostly with other disadvantaged students is exposed primarily to youngsters for whom immediate work and earnings are the most concrete need. While it may be easy for a given student to express his desire for a college education, there is little around him which suggests that his own friends and social equals regard such a thing to be possible. Since, as they move through the grades, students increasingly measure their behavior by the standards set and ac-

[15] Coleman *et. al. Equality of Educational Opportunity, op. cit.*

[16] *Racial Isolation in the Public Schools.* A Report of the U. S. Commission on Civil Rights. Washington, Government Printing Office, 1967.

cepted by their friends and associates, such a student is unlikely to follow through on his aspirations for college.[17]

Second, a similar process is probably involved in academic achievement. Students from poor backgrounds do not perform as well in school—even in the early grades— as more advantaged students. As was shown earlier, this performance gap increases as students move to higher grades. Students in schools where early and continuing academic difficulty is typical are likely to suffer from the cumulative disadvantage of their classmates. The students provide each other both with academic standards and varying degrees of academic interchange. Where the majority of students have low achievement, others will be likely to follow suit.

This was illustrated in testimony by David Jaquith, President of the Syracuse Board of Education, at the Commission hearing in Rochester. Explaining the positive effects of a transfer of disadvantaged students from Madison Junior High School to Levi, a junior high school which had a more advantaged student body, he said:

> . . . at Madison Junior High School, if you cooperated with the teacher and did your homework, you were a "kook."
>
> At Levi Junior High School, if you don't cooperate with the teacher and don't do your homework, you are a "kook." Peer pressure has tremendous effect on the motivation and motivation has a tremendous effect on achievement.[18]

In summary, there is a strong relationship between student and school social class, and performance and attitudes. The social class composition of schools is the single most important school factor affecting student performance and attitudes.[19]

Although the social class composition has a major effect on the performance of students in school, the racial composi-

[17] See Alexander and Campbell, "Peer Influence on Adolescent Aspirations and Achievements," *American Sociological Review*, p. 568 (1964).

[18] See Rochester Hearing, U. S. Commission on Civil Rights, pp. 473-474.

[19] U. S. Commission on Civil Rights, *op. cit.*, pp. 88-89.

tion also affects the performance of Negro students over and above the effect of social class. The Commission analyzed the possible explanations of this effect.

> These comparisons suggest a relationship between the performance of Negro students and the racial composition of classrooms. They do not, however, explain it. There are a number of possible explanations.
>
> First, there may be differences in the quality of education offered in a minority-Negro and majority-white school which accounts for the higher average Negro performance in majority-white schools.
>
> Second, it may be that there is a process of selection involved, whereby only initially more able Negro students attend majority-white schools.
>
> Finally, there may be student environment factors directly connected with racial composition which relate to the attitudes and performance of Negro Students.[20]

Further analysis of the data in the Office of Education survey and other studies led the commission to conclude that the variation in performance was not explained by the quality of the school program, quality of teaching, or selection of the students.

> It seems clear, however, that the performance of Negro students is distinctly less related to differences in the quality of schools and teachers than the social class and racial composition of their schools. This further reinforces the conclusion that the quality of education presently provided in schools does little to reverse the inequalities imposed upon children by factors within and outside the schools. The analysis thus suggests that changes in the social class or racial composition of schools would have a greater effect upon student achievement and attitudes than changes in school quality.[21]
>
> . . . The environment of schools with a substantial majority of Negro students, then, offers serious obstacles to learning. The schools are stigmatized as inferior in the

[20] *Ibid.*, p. 91.
[21] *Ibid.*, p. 100.

community. The students often doubt their own worth, and their teachers frequently corroborate these doubts. The academic performance of their classmates is usually characterized by continuing difficulty. The children often have doubts about their chances of succeeding in a predominantly white society and they typically are in school with other students who have similar doubts. They are in schools which, by virtue both of their racial and social class composition, are isolated from models of success in school.[22]

. . . Negro children in predominantly white schools more often score higher on achievement tests, develop higher aspirations, and have a firmer sense of control over their own destinies.

Differences in performance, attitudes, and aspirations occur most often when Negroes are in majority-white schools. Negro children in schools that are majority-Negro often fail to do better than Negro children in all-Negro schools. In addition, the results stemming from desegregated schooling tend to be most positive for those Negro children who began their attendance at desegregated schools in the earlier elementary grades.

An important contributing element to the damage arising from racially isolated schools is the fact that they often are regarded by the community as inferior institutions and students and teachers sense that their schools are stigmatized. This has an effect on their attitudes which influences student achievement.[23]

These studies demonstrate that the social class and racial composition of the schools and the associated school climate affect both the school achievement and attitudes of the students.

The conclusions of the *Equality of Educational Opportunity* study and the subsequent analysis in *Racial Isolation in the Public Schools* have been challenged by a number of critics. A major difficulty in studies of social-class and racial composition of the schools is separating the effects of other factors, such as difference in family background, previous learning, and

[22] *Ibid.*, p. 106.
[23] *Ibid.*, p. 114

quality of the school facilities and teachers, from the effect of social composition. The analysis made by the Commission on Civil Rights staff varied somewhat from analyses used by the U. S. Office of Education, but generally reinforced the finding that school composition is related to school performance. A number of studies using varying criteria of school performance and different methods of analysis have produced the same results.[24] Furthermore, longitudinal studies demonstrate that Negro students who have moved from segregated schools to integrated ones perform at higher levels than previously.[25] There is some evidence that white middle-class students also do better in integrated schools and no evidence that association with lower class or black students lowers their performance in any way. The present evidence consistently and clearly supports the conclusion that the racial and social class composition of the student bodies is associated with school achievement and other criteria of educational performance. Segregation in different schools can no longer be cited as advantageous for any group.

Extensive evidence supports the same conclusion regarding ability grouping or tracking for students with presumed differences in ability.[26] Although there are many studies of ability grouping and tracking, there is little evidence that such differentiated educational programs enhance the school

[24] See Thomas Pettigrew, "Race and Equal Educational Opportunity," *Harvard Educational Review* 38: 66-76, Winter 1968, for a review of this research.

[25] See A. B. Wilson study of Richmond, California in U. S. Commission on Civil Rights. *Racial Isolation in Public Schools*, Volume II, pp. 165-206, also his *Educational Consequences of Segregation in a California Community*, Berkeley, California, University of California Survey Research Center 1966; Report of White Plains, New York study, *New York Times*, October 22, 1967, p. E9; and Neal Sullivan's "Discussion" of Berkeley Study in *Harvard Educational Review* 38: 148-155, Winter 1968.

[26] See Walter R. Borg, "Ability Grouping in the Public Schools," 1966, Dembar Educational Research Services, Madison, Wisconsin; M. J. Eash, "Grouping: What Have We Learned?" *Educational Leadership*, 18: 429-434, 1961; and R. B. Ekstrom, "Experimental Studies of Homogeneous Grouping; a Critical Review," *School Review*, 69: 216-226, 1961; Miriam Goldberg, A. Harry Passow and Joseph Justman, *Effects of Ability Grouping*. Teachers College Press, New York: 1967, 254 pgs.

achievement of any group. When tracking involves different curricula, such as those that prepare for college entrance and those that provide only non-college preparatory courses, the outcome is certainly unequal. Students who have no opportunity to learn algebra, chemistry, or a foreign language will not have the same opportunity to further their education beyond high school as students with such high-school curricula. After a careful analysis of the evidence, the U. S. District Court held that the District of Columbia tracking system was a denial of equal opportunity on the same basis as racially or social class segregated schools.[27]

The theory of school learning which is reflected in the previous chapters of this book is, we believe, helpful in understanding the relation between school composition and school performance. The norms of expectations that prevail in school social systems define the level of school performance for the various groups of students. A student body or track composed predominantly of lower class or minority group students is usually associated with low academic expectations, while predominantly middle-class white schools or tracks are generally characterized by high expectations. Teachers verify the appropriateness of their expectations by the results of culturally biased tests of aptitude. They therefore evaluate the disadvantaged students as unable to learn the same as others. Educational programs are designed to fulfill the expectations of the teachers.[28]

As we noted in Chapter 4, the academic climate or norms of the school as defined by teacher, students, and other relevant groups is a crucial variable affecting the performance of students. If no one expects or considers it appropriate for students to learn well and all evaluate them as unable to learn, it is unlikely that many will perform at high levels. Such expectations are also communicated to students so they in turn come to define academic performance as inappropriate

[27] Hobson v. Hansen, *op. cit.*

[28] *See* Robert Rosenthal and Lenore Jacobson, *Pygmalion in the Classroom* (New York: Holt, Rinehart and Winston, 1968).

for them. If all their associates evaluate students in such groups as having low ability to learn, most will develop low self-concepts of ability and thus set low limits of school performance for themselves.

EDUCATION OF STUDENTS DISADVANTAGED BY RACE AND CLASS

Concern for the education of the disadvantaged has resulted in a number of programs, largely initiated and supported by the Federal government. The purpose of these programs is to compensate for educational disadvantages and enhance the education of those segments of our population that have not been adequately prepared for contemporary society. Included among these programs are the Head Start for pre-school youngsters, Upward Bound for disadvantaged older students, and a variety of activities financed under Title I of the Elementary and Secondary Act of 1965. The Job Corps and Manpower Retraining programs are designed to overcome the disadvantages of older youth and adult workers who have not received sufficient education to be productively employed in the society. All of these programs are intended to overcome the disadvantages that such groups have in school and employment and thereby compensate for the inequality in opportunity.

The difficulties involved in overcoming the segregation of inner-city children have led to many efforts to improve the education of these students without integration. It is extremely difficult to organize a large city school system so that all students attend schools composed of predominantly middle-class white students. Extensive busing, educational parks, and frequently permeation of school district boundaries are necessary to achieve appropriate balance of school populations. Programs designed to overcome the educational handicaps associated with segregation without integration have not resulted in great success.[29]

[29] U. S. Commission on Civil Rights. *Racial Isolation in Public Schools, op. cit.*, Chapter IV.

Most of the compensatory education undertaken has been based on the traditional belief that the failure to succeed in school results from the limitations of the individual student or the methods of teaching. The emphasis therefore has been to add staff and other resources to analyze the child's difficulties and remedy them through more individual attention and more intensive instructional methods. The concentration on analysis and instruction by teachers and educational specialists is not likely to produce effective school learning if the children do not associate with others who exhibit the desired type of learned behavior and who expect them to learn this behavior. Such children placed in a social environment where school achievement is the norm are much more likely to perform accordingly than if they are isolated from such learning environments regardless of the special resources and programs devised for them. If the norms or levels of expectation in lower class and Negro schools or tracks could be changed so that everyone—teachers, fellow students, and out-of-school groups—would expect such students to perform as middle-class white students generally do, greater achievement might result. Such changes in expectations are unlikely to occur under present theory and practice.

The traditional emphasis on fixed and limited abilities and the associated concept of individual differences tend to interfere with educating the disadvantaged. Education programs designed for the limited education of people who are mistakenly thought to be unable to acquire high quality education are more likely to perpetuate the disadvantages than to overcome them. The disadvantages of the poor or the Negro are not overcome by providing a type of education which guarantees that these people will not have the opportunity to move into other strata in society. Expansion of the programs for the education of the slow learners and the disadvantaged which have maintained the disadvantaged in the past will not overcome the disadvantages in the future.

The educational disadvantages of children from disadvantaged racial and social class groups are more likely to be overcome by providing them with the kinds of social-cultural environments in which they will learn the behavior that is necessary for the higher status or advantaged positions in society. Children from the disadvantaged sub-societies therefore must be provided the wide range of experiences that are common to the children from the educationally advantaged sub-groups. When such children have learned the prerequisite types of behavior, they may proceed with the high quality educational programs which characterize the schools which serve the children of the advantaged portions of our society. If the disadvantages are to be overcome, we must first create the kinds of social-cultural environments that have produced the advantaged or well-educated. They are not overcome by creating different and inferior educational environments. This suggests a different kind of emphasis than has characterized the efforts to educate the various types of disadvantaged in the past. Some compensatory types of socialization in the pre-school and early school years may be necessary; teachers and other associates must assume that the disadvantaged can learn and expect them to learn if equality of educational opportunity is to be achieved.

All this assumes that the society wishes to overcome the disadvantages and to provide the opportunity for disadvantaged children to enter the mainstream of American society. It is not yet clear that this is the goal of all Americans or of all educators. We have had an extended history of education designed to maintain various sorts of differences as well as efforts to reduce diversity. The former has been more characteristic of recent decades and our whole theory of individual differences and limited abilities has provided the basis for unequal educational programs. To provide equality we must develop a new theory of human abilities and draw upon our knowledge of the socialization process to design programs of education that will overcome the disadvantages of those against whom we have discriminated.

A society which professes to democratic ideals of equality of opportunity cannot endure with some educated and some denied the opportunity for the same education. The courts and Congress have defined the public policy of equality in educational opportunity. The society must now provide it or prepare for a heightened level of violent revolution.

SUGGESTED READINGS

EDWARDS, T. BENTLEY and FREDERICK M. WIRT. *School Desegregation in the North*, San Francisco: Chandler Publishing Co., 1967.

GOLDSTEIN, BERNARD, *Low Income Youth in Urban Areas*, New York: Holt, Rinehart and Winston, Inc., 1967. An excellent critical review of the literature on poverty and education.

McPARTLAND, JAMES, *The Segregated Student in Desegregated Schools*, Baltimore, Maryland: The Center for the Study of Social Organization of Schools, The Johns Hopkins University, 1968. Presents research showing that desegregation of classrooms and not schools is the crucial factor in upgrading lower class Negro students.

SEXTON, PATRICIA C. *Education and Income*, New York: The Viking Press, Inc., 1961. This book explores the relationships between income and educational opportunity and between social class and allocation of resources to children.

U.S. Commission on Civil Rights, *Racial Isolation in the Public Schools*, Washington, D.C., Supt. of Documents, U.S. Government Printing Office, 1967.

7

Educability
and the
Future Society

IN THIS BRIEF VOLUME we have been concerned with an examination of the social factors that produce variations in learning, with particular emphasis on the differences in learning that occur in school. In order to understand this, however, we have examined the variables affecting the differences in behavior learned between societies, as well as within a particular society. In these chapters, we have looked more specifically at those social factors which result in differences between individuals and groups within a relatively common social-cultural environment. We have, therefore, examined what in current educational jargon is known as "individual differences" in learning in the context of the social environment.

The variables which we have discussed in the previous chapters have all been known and have to various degrees been recognized in the examination of school learning. Although they may not have been identified in the particular categories and with the same concepts that we have used, teachers and educators have commonly discussed such factors as family background, social class identification, and the neighborhood from which a child comes in terms of differences in behavior and presumed learning ability. Although educators tend to be aware that social forces have an impact on learning, seldom have they systematically examined those social factors which produce differences in the behavior that is learned and presumed ability to learn.

We have indicated from time to time throughout this discussion that the programs planned for children in the school have been guided by a restrictive biological conception of school learning rather than by an expanding sociological or social-psychological conception. Some may question this assumption but we believe that the careful analysis of the manner in which teachers function and schools are organized substantiates our beliefs. In general, the primary belief we have criticized is that the amount and type of learning which occurs in schools is largely determined by relatively fixed and limited capacities or learning abilities. The student is perceived from this perspective as a person with certain constant capacities or abilities which are not subject to much change or expansion. Much of the school program is therefore organized to identify varying levels and types of abilities and to adapt the program of educational activities to particular fixed abilities of the children.

As a result of this basic, and what we believe to be fatal, assumption we have an extensive program of curriculum differentiation and a variety of grouping practices which are designed to fit the particular abilities of the students in the school. Teachers are constantly concerned with identifying and describing the abilities of individual students, and within the range of their courses, to evaluate the student's performance in the light of his ability, which is presumed to be relatively constant and limited. Such comments as "He is not working up to his capacity" or "He is doing as much as could be expected of him" or "He is an over-achiever" or "He is an under-achiever" are all reflections of the underlying assumption of fixed and limited abilities to learn. This basic framework for the organization and interpretation of educational processes might be identified as the intelligence or IQ complex in American education.

We have challenged this foundation for the educational program primarily by the analysis of social factors affecting school learning. Recent research on the biological foundation of learning also supports the thesis that environmental differences affect the brain structure. "Experiments . . . show that the memory-building experiences of an abundant, intellectually challenging life can enrich an animal's brain structure and chemistry—and that isolation and environmental impoverishment can impair it. Some . . . experiments even indicate that rats in an 'enriched environment may learn to solve many kinds of problems more effectively than deprived ones, and that animals reared in isolation perform more poorly.' If such findings are confirmed with humans as well as with other animals, the concept of limited biological ability may be greatly modified and the role of social environmental factors in learning may be expanded beyond the theses presented in this book. Certainly an understanding of the potential for improvement of education through the modification of the social environment for learning is essential for contemporary educators.

We have noted that the American educational practice has become dysfunctional for American society today. This is particularly true of the school allocation system which directs many into unskilled and unproductive social roles. Contemporary American society and projections into the immediate future indicate that we need an increasingly large proportion of the work force with high levels of educational achievement. We have noted that it is difficult to develop an educational program of the dimensions needed with a belief in limited and fixed capacities. The local school systems have not risen to the challenge of contemporary education without some inducements from outside sources. The needs of the society,

---

[1] David Perlman "The Search for the Memory Molecule," *The N.Y. Times Magazine* (July 7, 1968), p. 34. Perlman is here describing the work of David Krech, Mark Rosenzweig, and others at the University of California. *See also* David Krech.

however, are such that society is likely to develop new educational programs and foster the development of new beliefs on which to meet the expanded educational needs.

The federal education legislation of the 1960's is a manifestation of society's need for greatly expanded levels of education for increasing proportions of our young people. Much of this legislation has focused on expanding opportunities for higher education and programs for educating those segments of disadvantaged learners who have largely been discarded as uneducable at the higher levels. Thus, the federal government is mobilizing the resources of the society to promote the education of all citizens to the high levels needed in our society.

The task immediately ahead for American education is the mobilization of resources to develop educational environments in which higher and higher levels of learning will occur. Such learning environments are not likely to emerge from the beliefs which have characterized our educational system of the past decades. They rather necessarily will be based on a conception of essentially unlimited potential for educability. The biological and psychological specialists in learning have significant contributions to make to this educational system of the future. The sociologists, however, have an equally great contribution. The creation of social environments with new norms and beliefs about human behavior and new organizational patterns which will foster maximum learning must occur. The sociological conception of learning which we have sought to outline may provide the foundation for the creation of such educational environments. Certainly, the future needs of our society cannot be achieved through the perpetuation of the theories of infant damnation which have characterized the past notions of limited and fixed abilities to learn. New horizons of ever-expanding human educability must provide the foundation for the education of children in the twenty-first century.

Index

Ability grouping (*see* Tracking)
Ability self-concept, 15-16, 104-
  106
Academic achievement:
  expectation effect on, 95-97
  segregation effect on, 127-134
  and self-concept, 15-16, 105-
  106
Adolescents:
  groups, 64-70
  norms, 32, 68-69, 75-80
  significant others for, 64-97
  as a subculture, 41, 67-69
Advantaged and disadvantaged:
  expectations, 95
  present need for educational
    association of, 134-137
  school districts emphasize, 119-
  120
Afro-American culture, 51, 58
Agricultural occupation and early
    U. S. education, 10, 28, 47-49
Alexander, 129 fn
Allocation function of schools, 36-
  39, 140 (*see also* Tracking)
Alternate patterns of behavior, 20
American Indians:

federal government treatment,
  44-45, 49, 58
goals for education of, 42-43
subcultures of, 67
Americanization process, 41
Amish subculture, 49-50, 67, 68
Appalachia subculture, 47
Approval, 31-32, 33, 103-104
Ascribed groups, 64-65
Athletics:
  Negroes in, 116-117
  prowess in, 85-86, 87-89

Bandura, Albert, 14
Banneker program, 93-94
Behavior (*see also* Expectations,
    Self-concept structure)
  ability self-concept and, 15-16,
    104-106
  alternate patterns, 20
  common aspects, 19-26
  communication system, 23-24
  community living, 24
  control system, 25
  how acquired, 1-2, 26-36
  norms, 15, 64-97, 127, 141
  physical survival, 24

reassurance, 25-26
recreation, 25
reproduction, 24-25
segregated conditions, 127-134
specialties, 20-23, 26, 30
training, 24-25
universals, 19-23, 30
Bendix, Reinhard, 52 fn
Bernstein, Basil, 47 fn, 60 fn
Binet, Alfred, 6, 7
Biological foundation of learning
    (see Fixed intelligence con-
    cept)
Borg, Walter R., 132 fn
Brookover, Wilbur B., 12, 15, 54,
    55, 66, 71, 76, 92, 93, 94,
    105, 110 (all fn)
Bucket theory of intelligence, 8

California Test of Mental Maturity,
    12
Campbell, 129 fn
Canadian goals in education, 42
Carter, Robert, 119 fn
Cattell, 6
Civil Rights Acts (1954, 1964),
    125, 126, 128
Clark, Burton, 92 fn
Coleman, James S., 67 fn, 68-69,
    70 fn, 86-88, 90 fn, 116 fn,
    126 fn, 128 fn
College curriculum, 37, 84-85
Combs, Arthur W., 101
Commonality of behavior, 19-26
Common schools, 9, 34-35, 45, 46,
    116
Communication system, a universal,
    23-24, 100
Community living, a universal, 24
Compensatory programs, 94-95,
    125, 126, 134-137
Conflict thesis, adolescents vs.
    adults, 75
Contemporary educational needs,
    13, 38-39, 99, 115-137, 140-
    141

Control system, a universal, 25
Cooley, Charles H., 52 fn
Cuber, John F., 52 fn
Cultural shock, 21
Culture, 2, 19-39
    basic aspects, 23-26
    definition, 21-22
    deprivation, and subcultural
        variations, 55-62
    nature, 22-23
    transmission, 1-2, 26-36
Curriculum:
    college, 37, 84-85
    differentiation, 10-11, 35-38,
        45-46, 55, 61-62, 84-85, 116,
        118-119, 126 (see also Fixed
        intelligence concept)

Davis, Kingsley, 52 fn
Deaf children, institutionalized,
    and significant others, 107-
    109
De facto segregation, 44, 47, 119-
    121, 122-125
De jure segregation, 119
Desegregation (see Segregation)
Dewey, Richard, 66 fn
Differentiation of curriculum (see
    Curriculum differentiation)
Disadvantaged, 2, 55-62
    compensatory programs, 94-95,
        125, 126, 134-137
    contemporary educational
        needs, 13, 38-39, 99, 115-
        137, 140-141
    expectations from, 56, 90-91
    relation to school learning, 55-
        56, 59-62
District of Columbia school differ-
    entiation, 120-121, 124, 133
Dumont, Robert, Jr., 43 fn

Eash, M. J., 132 fn
Education:
    common vs. specialized, 9, 45-
        46

contemporary needs, 13, 38-39, 99, 115-137, 140-141
differentiated (*see* Tracking)
effect of segregation on equality, 116-121, 126, 136-137
formal, 26-28
informal, 26-28 (*see also* Socialization)
Japanese-American subculture and, 49, 59
Jewish subculture and, 59
local vs. centralized control, 44-45
major functions, 23
persistence of dysfunctional values, 12
relation to social stratification, 115-137
subcultural goals, 41-44
Educators, 13-14
Ekstrom, R. B., 132 fn
Elementary and Secondary Act of 1965, 134
Environment, effect on learning ability, 1-2, 14-17, 26-36, 99-100, 135-136, 140 (*see also* Fixed intelligence concept, Significant others, Socialization)
Equality of education, 116-137
Equality of Educational Opportunity study, 128-131
Erickson, Edsel L., 71, 76, 105, 106, 107, 110 (all fn)
Ethnic subcultural variations in U. S., 49-50
European immigrants to U. S., 34 35, 41-42, 43, 117
Expectations:
implications for academic achievement, 95-97
of school, from pupils, 33, 61-62, 83-91, 133-134
of significant others, 76-80, 83-93

Family group, as teachers, 29, 30
Family relationship, a universal, 24, 53
Faris, Robert, 14-15
Fixed intelligence concept, 3-17
and differentiated education, 35-36, 38, 55, 120, 126, 135
explanation for school failure, 9
history, 6-7, 9-11
and present-day needs, 13-17, 38-39, 99, 135, 139-140
and society expectations, 62, 92
Food beliefs, a universal, 25-26, 32
Formal and informal culture transmission (teaching), 26-36
Freedom-of-choice attendance plans, 125
Friends:
achievement expectations, 77-80
significant others, 72, 73, 74, 76

Galton, Francis, 6, 7
Goffman, Irving, 81 fn
Goldberg, Miriam, 132 fn
Goldhamer, Herbert, 52 fn
Gordon, Milton, 52 fn
Gottlieb, David, 15, 54, 66, 92 (all fn)
Goud, Nelson, 88 fn
Groups, 2, 64-97
adolescent, 64-70
ascribed, 64-65
norms, 15, 64-97
reference, 65-66
significant others, 66, 68-80
and subcultures, 41
voluntary, 64-65

Haarer, David, 106 fn
Hamachek, Don E., 94, 105, 110 (all fn)
Hansen, Carl, 120, 121, 124, 133 (all fn)

Harding, Kenneth A., 106 fn
Havighurst, Robert, 60 fn
Head Start, 134
Heredity and intelligence (*see* Fixed
    intelligence concept)
Herriot, Robert E., 91 fn
Hobson, Julius W., 120, 121, 124,
    133 (all fn)
Hostetler, John, 67 fn
Human behavior (see Behavior)
Humber, W. J., 66 fn
Hunt, J. McV., 3-5, 6, 7, 8-9, 11-12

Immigrants to U. S., 34-35, 41-42,
    43, 117
Individual:
    learning ability, 1-17, 26-36,
        99-100, 135-136, 140
    relation to behavior arena, 2,
        27, 99-113
Industrialization and early educa-
    tion, 10
Institutions, total, 80-81
Intelligence:
    alternate theories, 12-17
    bucket theory, 8
    fixed, prevailing concept, 3-17
        (*see* Fixed intelligence con-
        cept)
    measurement, 3-13
Intermarriage, 51
IQ complex, 11-12, 140

Jacobson, Lenore, 62 fn, 83, 92,
    94, 133 fn
Japanese-American subculture, 49,
    59
Jewish subculture, 49
Job Corps, 134
Joiner, Lee M., 71, 76, 105, 106,
    107 (all fn)
Justman, Joseph, 132 fn

Kahl, Joseph, 52 fn
Kariger, Hugh, 55 fn

Kenkel, William F., 52 fn
Kinch, John W., 109 fn
Knowledge (*see* Learning)

Language:
    common, major bond, 21, 23-
        24, 32
    correct vs. colloquial, 30-32
    culture transmission, 22, 27-28,
        35
    perception factor, 100
    and self-concept, 100-101
    of subculture, and school learn-
        ing, 59-61
Learning:
    and behavior norms, 2, 15-17
    conception of, present study,
        15-17
    culture, 26-27
    and individual ability, 1-17, 26-
        36, 99-100, 135-136, 140
Legislation on segregation, 116-117,
    119-129
LePere, Jean M., 94, 105, 110 (all
    fn)
Leu, Don, 55 fn
Linton, Ralph, 19 fn, 20, 23 fn
Lipset, Seymour, 52 fn
Lower-class strata (*see also* Disad-
        vantaged)
    expectations of parents, 79
    jobs and income, 51
    in school situation, 55-56, 59-
        62, 115-137

McDill, Edward, 90-91
Male vs. female role in society, 20,
    21, 26, 30
Manpower retraining programs, 134
Maslow, Abraham, 101
Mead, G. H., 65 fn
Measurement of intelligence, 3-13
    and rural areas, 47-49
    and socioeconomic strata, 55
Measurement specialists, 5, 8-9,
    11-12

Mendieta y Nunez, Lucio, 52 fn
Mentally retarded, 12-13, 105-106
Mexican-Americans, a subculture, 50, 53
Meyers, Edmund, Jr., 90-91
Migrant workers, 50
Myrdal, Gunnar, 116 fn

Negroes:
    and athletics, 117-118
    biological classification, 51
    goals for education of, in U. S., 43
    and majority goal, 58, 136-137
    race stratification, and education, 115-137
    and school learning, 61
    and social system, 51-52, 115-137
    a subculture, 51

Parents:
    and individual's self-concept, 107-109, 110-112
    as significant others, 71-80, 107-109
Parsons, Talcott, 52 fn
Passow, A. Harry, 132 fn
Perception, factor in socialization, 100, 107-109
Perlman, David, 140 fn
Pettigrew, Thomas, 132 fn
Physical survival, a universal, 24
Piaget, J., 14
Plessy-Ferguson decision, 116
Psychology:
    controlled-situation experimentation, 13-14
    self-concept theory, 101
Pupil-teacher relationship, 81-93, 103-104, 107-109

Quantity concept, and fixed intelligence theory, 7-8

Racial composition of class, effect on performance, 129-130

Racial stratification and education, 115-137
Racial subcultural variations in U. S., 50-52
Reassurance, a universal, 25-26
Recreation, a universal, 25
Reference groups, 16, 64-65, 68, 96-97
Regional subcultural variations in U. S., 46-47
Religion, a universal, 21, 25
Reproduction, a universal, 24-25
Reward, teaching method, 31-32, 33, 103-104
Rigsby, Leo, 90-91
Rogers, Carl R., 101
Role conflict, 66
Rosenthal, Robert, 62 fn, 83, 92, 94, 133 fn
Rural subculture:
    goals for education of, 43-44
    group interaction, 69
    variations from urban subculture, 47-49

St. John, Nancy Hoyt, 91 fn
School learning and subcultural diversity, 56-62
Schools:
    allocation function, 36-39, 140 (see also Tracking)
    closed system, 80-81
    common, 9, 34-35, 45, 46, 116
    district organization, segregation factor, 43-44, 121
    local control vs. centralized, 44-45
    variations between, 32, 89-91
    variations within, 90, 91-93
Segregation:
    changes in public policy, 121-127
    de facto, 44, 47, 119-121, 122-125
    de jure, 119
    district policy, 43-44, 121

effect on student performance,
127-134
and equality of opportunity,
116-121, 126, 136-137
graduate facilities, 121-122
legislation, 116-117, 119-129,
141
types, 119-121
Self-concept, 99-113
of ability, 15-16, 104-106
definition, 100-101
enhancing, 109-113
and expectations, 133-134
reciprocal nature, 103
relation to individual role, 101-
106
relation to parents, 107-109,
110-112
relation to teachers, 81-83,
103-104, 107-109
sociological perspective of, 102
Separate-but-equal doctrine, 116,
121-122
Sex roles, a universal, 24-25
Shils, Edward, 52 fn
Significant others:
adolescent-group, 64-97
behavior norms, 15-16
and deaf institutionalized
children, 107-109
definition, 2
effect of evaluation of, 76-77
friends, 71-80
identification, 68-76, 96-97
implication for education, 93-97
parents, 71-80, 107-109
teachers, 81-83, 103-104, 107-
109
Smith, Mildred, 94 fn
Snygg, Donald, 101
Social factors:
and educability, 138-141
effect on student performance,
128-132
stratification, 51-55, 115-137

Social interaction theory, 15-17
Socialization, informal (see also
Significant others)
applied to academic behavior,
32-33, 135-136
characteristics, 29-32
common vs. differentiated,
34-36
effectiveness as teaching
method, 1-2, 26-36
influence, 1-2, 99-100, 135-136
Social organizations (see Groups)
Society:
basic components, 15
common aspects of behavior,
19-26
definition, 21-22
differences in, 2, 40-41, 46-56
diverse behavior, 19-23, 41-62
goals in relation to subculture
goals, 56-58, 66-68, 136-137
nature, 22-23
role in, a universal, 24
survival, 24-25
Socioeconomic status:
expectations of school, 90-91
subcultural variations, 52-55
Sociologists and education, 14-15,
141
Spanish-speaking subculture, 50
Specialization in curriculum (see
Curriculum differentiation)
Specialties, 20-23, 26, 30
Student expectations, 83-89
Subcultures:
adolescent, 41, 64-97
and education, 40-62
goals, relation to dominant
group goals, 56-58, 66-68,
136-137
maintained by U. S. educational
policy, 117
U. S. goals for, 41-44
variations in U. S., 40-44, 46-
56

Subsociety (*see* Subculture)
Sullivan, Neal, 132 fn
Surveillance, effect on expectations,
    76, 77-78
Symbolic interaction, 100

Tannenbaum, Abraham J., 88
Teacher:
    of deaf children, 107-109
    everyone a, 29
    expectations, 33, 61-62, 83-91,
        133-134
    pupil relationship, 81-83, 103-
        104, 107-109
Teaching:
    continuous process, 30-31
    formal and informal transmis-
        sion of culture, 26-36
Thomas, Shailer, 94, 105, 110
    (all fn)
Total institutions, 80-81
Towne, Richard E., 106 fn
Tracking:
    in District of Columbia schools,
        120-121, 124, 133
    U. S. education concept, 10-11,
        37, 45-46, 55, 61-62, 84-85,
        113, 118-119, 120, 126, 132-
        137
Training, a universal, 24-25

Universals, 19-26, 30
Upward Bound, 134
Urban vs. rural education, 43-44
U. S. Commission on Civil Rights,
    128, 129-132, 134 fn
U. S. subcultural variations, 46-56
    ethnic, 49-50
    patterns of behavior, 20
    racial, 50-52
    regional, 46-47
    rural-urban, 47-49
    socioeconomic, 52-55

Values (norms), effect of social
    environment, 1, 15, 64-97
Variable learning abilities concept
    (*see* Fixed intelligence
    concept)
Vocational education (*see* Tracking)
Voluntary groups, 64-65

Waller, Willard, 81-83
Walters, Richard, 14
Wax, Murray, 43 fn
Wax, Rosalie, 43 fn
Weber, Max, 52 fn
Wilson, A. B., 132 fn
Woodring, Paul, 120 fn
Wright, J. Skelly, 119 fn, 120, 121,
    123, 124, 125
Wylie, Ruth C., 106 fn